JACQUI HAYWARD

MEMOIRS
OF LANCASTER GUNNER

HAROLD SYDNEY HAYWARD

Tekline Publishing
Books that make you think

COPYRIGHT

Copyright © 2019 by Jacqui Hayward

All rights reserved. No part of this publication may be reproduced, distributed, or transmitted in any form or by any means, including photocopying, recording, or other electronic or mechanical methods, without the prior written permission of the publisher, except for the purposes of brief quotations embodied in critical reviews or for the reporting of current events (this does not apply to photographs) and certain other noncommercial uses permitted by copyright law.

Fair use is permitted. Fair use allows the limited use of copyrighted material without permission from the copyright holder for purposes such as criticism, parody, news reporting, research and scholarship, and teaching.

Permission is granted to reproduce for personal and educational use only.

First Printing, August 2019

ISBN 9781686782367
Tekline Publishing
ENGLAND

PICTURE CREDITS AND DISCLAIMER

Unless stated otherwise, the photos and artwork in this book originate from Public Domain or is covered by Creative Common licenses.

The cover picture is based upon the Memorial Avro Lancaster Mk X bomber with the view of dorsal twin .50 Browning gun turret. It was taken by Andrew Mynarski, from Thunder Bay, Canada on 30 July 2010 and has made available under the Creative Commons Attribution-Share Alike 2.0 Generic license. According to that license:

You are free:
to share - to copy, distribute and transmit the work to remix - to adapt the work

Under the following conditions:

attribution - You must give appropriate credit, provide a link to the license, and indicate if changes were made. You may do so in any reasonable manner, but not in any way that suggests the licensor endorses you or your use. The link to the license is as follows:

https://creativecommons.org/licenses/by-sa/2.0/deed.en

ACKNOWLEDGMENTS

Although no longer with us, I would like to pay tribute to my wonderful dad and hope he would be pleased that his children, grandchildren and future generations will be able to read his story, he will not be forgotten!

Special thanks to my mum, who passed away three years after dad died. She encouraged dad to talk about his life and made notes about the stories he sometimes reluctantly told, without her patience and perseverance there would have been no starting point for this book.

Also, I thank Historian Graham Osborne who took on the task over many months of researching all aspects of dads military history, this even included a trip to Germany! He did a fantastic job but said it had been a privilege to work on this project. Without Graham's input, the book would not have been possible.

Likewise, my husband Julian who used his IT skills to enhance photos and support me when technology got the better of me!

Finally I would like to thank my cousin Fred Harding, without him this book would not have been possible. He painstakingly undertook the task of putting all aspects of this book together, I just provided the material. He has brought my dad's story to life and this book will remain a family treasure for many years to come.

DEDICATION

I would like to dedicate this book to our darling grandchildren Xander, Ayla and Mila and any future Grandchildren

MEMORIAL

As many as 125,000 aircrew served Britain in Bomber Command during the Second World War. 57,205 died for that cause, 8,403 were wounded in action and, like my dad, 9,838 became prisoners of war. A total of 75,446 airmen (60% of operational airmen) were killed, wounded or taken prisoner. It is my hope that my dad's story will be a lasting reminder and a memorial to the courage and sacrifice that these brave men shared in defending our great country. They should never be forgotten.

CONTENTS

Copyright
Picture Credits
Acknowledgements
Dedication
Memorial
Preface
1. Training and Dad's First Posting
2. France and Back
3. The Channel Islands
4. Pushed From Pillar to Post
5. Air Gunner Sergeant Hayward
6. Dad Goes a Gardening
7. Baptism of Fire
8. The Letter
9. Inside Stalag IV-B
Epilogue
Appendix - Dad's Memorabilia
Author Biography
Dad and the Radio of Evil

PREFACE

This book is based upon the memoirs of my dad, Harold Sydney Hayward, which tell of his exploits as a Lancaster Bomber Gunner in the Royal Air Force between 25 February 1939 and 31 July 1945. My dad had always been reluctant to talk about what happened during this period for reasons which will become evident as you read this book.

It is thanks to my mum, Emily Hayward, who over the years, was able to prise out from my dad what happened to him during those years and she kept notes of what he said. Mum's notes were kept among our family memorabilia which included, photos and papers, which I uncovered when mum died on 10 March 2003 which was almost three years later to the day when dad died, on 12 March 2000.

Having read my mum's notes, I believe my dad's story is a story that must be told and preserved for posterity, not only for him but for the thousands of young men, aged between 19 and 25, who died taking the fight to the enemy until ground forces could be mobilised for D-Day, June 1944.

My dad's story gives a first-hand account of what Bomber Command aircrews actually went through and although a memorial in Green Park in London was unveiled by Queen Elizabeth II on 28 June 2012 to highlight the heavy casualties suffered by the aircrews during the war, this is a poor substitute for the words of someone who was there in the thick of it and who lived to tell his story. This was my dad.

Historians will tell you that Bomber Command aircrews suffered a terrible casualty rate. Of a total of 125,000 aircrew, 57,205 were killed. That is a 46-percent death rate. A further 8,403 were wounded in action and 9,838 became prisoners of war. Therefore, a total of 75,446 airmen (60 percent of operational airmen) were killed, wounded or taken prisoner. Nonetheless, the aircrews flew a total of 364,514 operational sorties but with 8,325 aircraft lost in action.

It is sad that so many young men died fighting for our freedom but memories of them will not be lost if you read this book, because my dad's story is just as much their story as it is his. Upon uncovering my dad's memoirs through my mum's notes, I procured the services of aviation historian, Graham N Osborn, to corroborate my dad's story. He obtained my dad's service record, researched the historical records and for the most part, corroborated dad's story.

It is true that there were several discrepancies where research produced some information that is in variance with that offered by my dad, but Mr Osborn acknowledged that official documents often produced anomalies and therefore he said that one should not place too much importance to the discrepancies between the testimony of my dad and that of the official records.

Before proceeding with my dad's story in Bomber Command, I would like to spend a little time to tell you about him through the words of my son Adam who, in 2003, wrote about his grandad in a school history project. It was called,"The True Life Story and Adventures of Warrant Officer Harold Sydney Hayward, by his Grandson Adam Norfolk, July 2003." I shall use Adam's story to provide the framework upon which this book will be constructed. My son begins as follows:

My grandfather, Harold Sydney Hayward was born on the 31 July 1920 in Walton On The Naze. His father died when he was six months old as a result of gas poisoning in the First World War. Consequently his mother remarried and my grandfather was sent to live with his grandfather who was my great, great grandfather. Edward Hayward was a very strict and religious man and my grandfather did not have a happy childhood. He's aim was to leave his grandfather's home as soon as possible.

In the year 1938 upon noticing an advert in the newspaper requiring volunteers for regular service, my grand father wrote to the address and was sent a form to fill in.

After waiting a few weeks, he was asked to attend the R.A.F Headquarters in Kingsway London, for a medical examination and educational test. Following another period of waiting, he was over the moon when eventually informed that he had been accepted as aircraft hand 2nd class general duties.

It is from this brief abstract from Adam's school project that my dad's story in the RAF begins.

Chapter 1
TRAINING AND DAD'S FIRST POSTING

In the spring of 1939, dad was sent to west Drayton to join up with more recruits where they were sorted into groups of about forty and then dispatched off to various training squadrons. Dad was required to report to No. 1 Training Depot Royal Air Force Station Uxbridge on the morning of Friday, 24 February 1939.

From information I have obtained through the services of Mr Osborn my dad would have spent the first day going through the induction process, which included, medical examination, completing next of kin and other documentation and being issued with Rank and Service Number 635625. Later that day the new recruits would be marched to the clothing stores where each man was issued with a uniform and other basic kit.

There would have been no fitting or trying on of the uniform but having been marched back to their barracks each man would have been told to "dress up" for inspection and the camp tailor would then have chalked up any alterations to be made. For the next few days, the recruits would have paraded in civilian clothes until their uniforms were returned.

Towards the end of the day, they were given some writing paper and envelopes and told to write to their parents, loved ones, etc. So military life began.

General Duties Service Entrant 635625 Aircraftman Second Class (NC2) Harold Sidney Hayward now began twelve weeks of basic military training. The inevitable "square bashing" military drill, discipline, lectures, physical training and general introduction to the Royal Air Force way of life would also have included trade assessment tests. A typical daily routine for new entrants would be as follows:

06.30 Reveille. 10 minutes to dress into PT (Physical Training) kit for 15 minutes of strenuous exercise. Back to the barracks, make bed and wash and shave. **07.15** March to the dining Hall for breakfast.

07.45 Marched back to the barracks. Clean Boots; tidy bed space for inspection.

08.00 On parade for inspection.

08.10 Parade Drill.

09.00 Marched to lecture rooms.

10.30 Tea Break.

10.45 Resume lectures.

12.00 Marched to the Dinning Hall for lunch.

13.00 Classroom or workshop practise.

15.00 Tea Break.

15.15 Resume classes.

17.00 Marched to the Dinning Hall for tea.

17.30 Return to Barracks. Writing up notes. Cleaning Kit. Writing Letters.

20.00 NAAFI opened. Billiards, Table Tennis , Darts. Tea, Coffee, biscuits, and cake but no alcohol.

21.00 Return to barracks.

21.15 "Stand by your beds" for evening roll call.

21.30 Lights out.

Wednesday and Saturday afternoons were compulsory sports periods and Saturday morning was set aside for domestic chores such as scrubbing bedside lockers, polishing bed space, cleaning windows, washrooms and so on. On Sunday at 09.00 there was the compulsory church parade followed by barrack inspection by the Commanding Officer. However, the afternoon was given over for free time but like the other recruits dad was confined to camp and so on and so forth, with slight variations, for the next twelve weeks.

On the day before the completion of his basic military training at Uxbridge dad was chosen with about a hundred other men from Hornchurch and other squadrons to represent the R.A.F. as guards of honour alongside members of the army and the royal navy on the first day of the Royal Tournament which was held between 18 May -3 June 1939. They were proudly inspected by Prince George, 1st Duke of Kent and Princess Marina of Greece, Duchess of Kent.

Following the traditional "passing out" parade on Friday, 19 May 1939 dad was issued with a weekend leave pass and railway travel warrant to his hometown. Like all trainee aircrew who completed their training dad was presented with the aircrew brevet, an outward symbol that he was fully qualified to carry out his duties. It was just a question as to what job he was best suited to do now that he had graduated. It happened that during his training dad had some rudimentary training as an Operations Room Assistant. As a result he was posted to RAF Hornchurch, located to the southeast of Romford, as a table plotter.

RAF Hornchurch was home to 65 Spitfire Squadron and was a Sector Station controlling Sector D in 11 Group Fighter Command that was organised round the Dowding System of fighter control. Dad was placed under the command of Group Captain John Beville Howard Nicholas and received the pay of 3 shillings (15 pence) per day. A further sum of 6d (2.5p) was set aside as a post-war credit.

Captain Nicholas would distinguish himself when over Dunkirk on 26th May 1940 when he destroyed a Me109 and damaged a Me109 and a Me110. During the Battle of Britain, he damaged a Do17 on 24th July and shared in probably destroying a Me109 on 14th August. He would go on to be posted to Australia in 1944 where he took command of 54 Squadron at Darwin in June. He led the squadron until its disbandment on 31st October 1945. Nicholas returned to the UK in November and on 5th February 1946 he went to a staff job at HQ 11 Group. He stayed in the RAF on an Extended Service Commission and resigned in July 1949 as a Flight Lieutenant. He died in April 1993 in London.

The inside of the Hornchurch operations room was more impressive than its exterior facade suggested. The entrance to the operations room was at the top of a short flight of stairs, which gave access to a built up timber platform running down the left-hand side of the room known as the dais.

This wide raised area looked down from a height of about four feet onto the centre of the room. Here sat nearest the door the Ops. (Operations) B Officer who was assistant to the Ops Controller. To the left of "Ops B" was a Leading Aircraftman and to his left was an Aircraftman wearing a headset and breastplate telephone set.

In the centre of the dais, a section of the floor was raised by a further six inches, and it was here that the Senior Controller sat, in 1939 a Flight Lieutenant but later this position was filled by a Squadron Leader. Further again to the left, against the windows sat an Army Officer, whose duty was to keep liaison between the Anti-aircraft (AA) guns and the RAF. He had two army signallers to assist him. Along the front of the dais was a built-in desk containing clearly marked telephone keys providing communication between the Operations Room Group Headquarters, the various squadrons, aircraft and other units.

Behind the dais, three windows gave access to the wireless operators who sat in sound proofed cubicles so as to preserve the quiet of the Operations Room. The wireless operators maintained contact with the aircraft in the air and switched the R/T (Radiotelephone) through to the controller or his assistants in response to a pressed switch on the control desk.

From the centre of this dais, the controllers overlooked two plotting tables. The main plotting table positioned centrally and to the right displayed the plots of incoming raids and alongside it and to the left, a smaller table had the movements of the Hornchurch and other sector fighters displayed on it. The large plotting table had a representation of the outline map of Southeast England drawn as a black outline on white ground. The smaller table was displayed as white outline on a black background. It was at these tables that dad worked as part of a team under the direction of a Sergeant.

Dad's job involved plotting enemy air craft and their position as the information was being relayed by telephone through their phones from the radar stations posted at intervals along the coast.

As dad carried out his duties he was well aware that tensions were high on the airbase. This was because, since March 1939, Germany had been carving up what little that remained of Czechoslovakia and it was clear to both the British and French Governments that their policy of appeasement was no longer working.

Belatedly, the British and French Military Chiefs met to devise a common defence policy against the Axis powers. If Hitler was to invade Poland, it was recognised that Britain and France would be drawn into war with Germany, a war that nobody wanted. Nonetheless, it was necessary to make preparations for all eventualities, including war.

The decision was taken that a British Expeditionary Force (BEF), together with an Air Component and an Advanced Air Striking Force (AASF) of Bomber Command should be sent to France, to support the French forces. The French would give the British Squadrons full facilities on French airfields provided that their aircraft would not be used for the unrestricted bombing of German targets from these bases.

This far from satisfactory arrangement produced months of disagreement between the British and French governments with all the attendant delay.

A solution to the problem had still not been found when on the 1 September 1939 Hitler invaded Poland as had been feared. On Sunday, 3rd September 1939, Prime Minister Neville Chamberlain announced on the radio that Britain was at war with Germany.

Sunderland Daily Echo and Shipping Gazette | 3 September 1939

Neville Chamberlain's Declaration of War

I am speaking to you from the Cabinet Room at 10, Downing Street.

This morning the British Ambassador in Berlin handed the German Government a final note stating that unless we heard from them by 11 o'clock, that they were prepared at once to withdraw their troops from Poland, a state of war would exist between us.

I have to tell you now that no such undertaking has been received, and that consequently this country is at war with Germany.

You can imagine what a bitter blow it is to me that all my long struggle to win peace has failed. Yet I cannot believe that there is anything more or anything different that I could have done and that would have been more successful.

Up to the very last it would have been quite possible to have arranged a peaceful and honourable settlement between Germany and Poland, but Hitler would not have it.

He had evidently made up his mind to attack Poland whatever happened; and although he now says he put forward reasonable proposals which were rejected by the Poles, that is not a true statement.

The proposals were never shown to the Poles nor to us; and though they were announced in a German broadcast on Thursday night, Hitler did not wait to hear comments on them, but ordered his troops to cross the Polish frontier the next morning.

His action shows convincingly that there is no chance of expecting that this man will ever give up his practice of using force to gain his will. He can only be stopped by force, and we and France are today, in fulfillment of our obligations, going to the aid of Poland, who is so bravely resisting this wicked and unprovoked attack upon her people. We have a clear conscience. We have done all that any country could do to establish peace. The situation in which no word given by Germany's ruler could be trusted and no people or country could feel itself safe has become intolerable.

And now that we have resolved to finish it, I know that you will all play your part with calmness and courage.

At such a moment as this the assurances of support which we have received from the Empire are a source of profound encouragement to us.

When I have finished speaking certain detailed announcements will be made on behalf of the Government. Give these your close attention.

The Government have made plans under which it will be possible to carry on the work of the nation in the days of stress and strain that may be ahead. But these plans need your help.

You may be taking your part in the fighting services or as a volunteer in one of the branches of civil defence. If so you will report for duty in accordance with the instructions you receive.

You may be engaged in work essential to the prosecution of war for the maintenance of the life of the people - in factories, in transport, in public utility concerns or in the supply of other necessaries of life. If so, it is of vital importance that you should carry on with your jobs.

Now may God bless you all and may He defend the right, for it is evil things that we shall be fighting against - brute force, bad faith, injustice, oppression and persecution - and against them I am certain that the right will prevail.

Neville Chamberlain
Prime Mininster

With Britain now at war it would not be long before my dad would be right in the thick of it

Chapter 2
FRANCE - THERE AND BACK

When Chambelain declared war on Germany, RAF Hornchurch was already on a war footing. According to the Hornchurch Airdrome Historical Trust, as early as September of 1938 the airbase had been brought to a state of immediate readiness for war and all personnel were recalled from leave and the operations room was manned 24 hours a day. These measures were escalated because of the seriousness of Adolf Hitler's claims being made over the region of Czechoslovakia called Sudetenland in that year.

> *As a prelude to the possible future hostilities which would now include RAF Hornchurch, they could only sit and wait for the outcome of what looked increasingly likely as being another world war. When 1939 finally arrived, the first outstanding event to take place at the aerodrome was the re-equipment of all three home squadrons with the new Supermarine Spitfire, the first instalment happened on 13th February when 74 squadron received their Spitfires. Over the next eight weeks, 54 and 65 squadrons were to make the changeover from their Gloster Gladiators to the new monoplane fighter.* (Hornchurch Airdrome Historical Trust)

Two hours after Chambelain's declaration of war with Germany, the air-raid sirens were sounded at Hornchruch as unidentified aircraft was plotted approaching the base. All off duty personnel complete with helmets and gas masks were ordered into the air-raid shelters while dad and his colleagues plotted the aircraft heading for the base.

Spitfires were scrambled to intercept the incoming aircraft only to find that the unidentified aircraft were French planes which had strayed off course following the activation of the British Expeditionary Force (BEF) Air Component part of the RAF Advanced Air Striking Force (AASF), only a few hours before. Needless to say, there was relief all around but the incident proved that the airbase was fully operational, ready to tackle potential threats that came their way.

Spitfires scramble from RAF Hornchurch (September 1940)
Picture Credit: Film Inspector

As for dad, it soon became evident that the RAF had other plans for him. His plotting role at Hornchurch was quickly taken over by members of the Women in the Air Force, WAFs, and within a few days of the incident, dad was reassigned to 23 Wing Signals Unit in the newly formed 60 Fighter Wing as an Operations Room Plotter. The only problem was that 23 Wing Signals Unit was located in France.

In late September 1939, after a short overnight stay at RAF Northolt dad was transported to Heston aerodrome where he joined about forty other RAF personnel destined for posts in France.

The transfer to France was in an Armstrong Whitworth Ensign airliner, one of several that were operating a twice-daily service between Heston and Le Bourget in Northern France. Just a few days before these large four engine airliners had been in the service of Imperial Airways flying affluent travellers to Europe. The plane had been stripped of its seats to make more room for men and cargo, so they travelled sitting on the floor.

It was a most uncomfortable flight and everyone was relieved when they arrived at their destination, Le Bourget. From here dad was transferred by road transport to Allonville, approximately six miles from Amein where 23 Wing Signal Unit had established a sector operations room in a large country chateau.

It was from this chateu that dad and others were to control the fighters of 60 Fighter Wing who were now located on an airfield at Lille-Seclin, about sixty miles from Allonville.

Hawker Hurricanes of No. 85 Squadron RAF, stand at readiness at Lille-Seclin, 1940
Picture Credit: Imperial War Museum (C 1156) and is in the Public Domain

For a few months dad carried out his duties plotting the movements of the fighters of 60 Fighter Wing, but as more squadrons and men were committed to the defence of France, this expansion of RAF operations within the BEF the wing status soon became redundant. As a consequence 60 Wing was disbanded on the 16 January 1940.

Four days later dad and others of his unit, together with their equipment, were reassigned to the Headquarters of the newly formed 14 Fighter Group located at Achicourt, a French city located north of France, close to and south-west of Arras. This move had little impact on the day-to-day operational aspects of plotting the movements of allied aircraft.

It was summer time when dad arrived at Achicourt, so it wasn't too bad being housed in tents though there were six or eight men to each tent (bell tents). However winter approached and that year was a particularly freezing cold winter! Dad and his RAF colleagues were transferred to the loft of a farm building, but because there was no felting under the old fashioned clay tiles, the snow just blew straight through onto the men trying to sleep, all fully clothed and complete with balaclavas. As for the beds, they consisted of straw filled bags laid on three wooden boards, which were placed onto a trestle, these straw beds were called pallia's. They were basic, but dad did say in his memoirs that they were thankful that at least they would not be lying directly on the concrete floor! The food was served in a room below, which led off from the kitchen.

Apart from the group which consisted of approximately thirty men, there were also about one hundred and fifty Airmen from transport who came from various different areas to eat there. The food was served in shifts and although the food wasn't special, there was always plenty of bread, tinned food and margarine. Their pay was pretty good, as at the time, the exchange rate was high, so they could afford to eat away from the farm. Fortunately, their lived next door a middle-aged Belgium couple who used to cook very good meals for the boys for a minimal charge for around twelve francs for a meal.

During this period, the work dad and his co-workers did took place in a Nissen hut, which was situated about half a mile from the farm. Here they would have stayed having had it not been for Hitler's invasion of France on 10 May 1940. As the German forces swept aside all opposition and was heading in their direction, it became clear that 14 Group could no longer operate.

On the 19 May, the order was given for 14 Group to evacuate to Dunkirk and the men were allowed to take with them only those items that could be carried, everything else would have been destroyed or disabled and this included most of the operational records held by 14 Group.

Dad's group headed for Dunkirk in a convoy of twelve lorries, however on the journey through France, they were strafed by German planes. Dad said that everyone dived smartly into a very convenient ditch and fortunately there were no casualties, but then a message was received saying that Dunkirk had been cut off by the enemy. The lorries were therefore diverted to Boulogne, where dad's group were joined by a few Army personnel from Dunkirk. They reached Boulogne on 21 May 1940, just before the Germans closed in and surrounded the town.

Boulogne was chaotic to say the least. There were masses of men all over the docks area and not all got on to the ferry, though hundreds did manage to.

Dad and his group managed to get on the ferry, The Canterbury, "crammed in the bow of the ferry - a bit like sardines," he said. A notable war service saw the ship deliver troops to Calais and Boulogne not long before both ports fell, then being present at both Dunkirk and D Day. (HHVFerry Blog).

The Canterbury leaving Boulogne. World War II the ship evacuated troops from Calais and Boulogne not long before both ports fell, then was present at both Dunkirk and D Day.
Picture Credit: HHVFerry Blog (Public Domain)

The lorries had been destroyed to prevent them from being used by the enemy. Dad later found out that the French and remaining British troops held out at Boulogne until 25 May when they finally surrendered. Calais was taken the next day, leaving Dunkirk as the only viable port from which the British Expeditionary Force, part of the French army and the remains of the Belgian army could escape. Meanwhile, dad's ferry had reached Dover and dad gratefully disembarked on British soil.

Thousands of members of the armed forces were not so lucky. They were stuck on the beach of Dunkirk awaiting their fate at the hands of the Germans. But as the German forces closed in on the last pocket of BEF resistance, the Royal Navy implemented "Operation Dynamo", the evacuation of Dunkirk. This became known as the Miracle of Dunkirk, when between 26 May and 3 June 1940 and aided by about 850 small craft manned by private individuals, 338,226 British, Belgium and French forces were evacuated to England.

This in itself was a miracle but strange things happened which made it possible. The first was that for some reason, which has never yet been fully explained, Hitler overruled his generals and halted the advance of his armoured columns at the very point when they could have proceeded to the British army's annihilation. They were now only ten miles away!

Second, a storm of unprecedented fury broke over Flanders on Tuesday, 28 May (1940) grounding the German Luftwaffe squadrons. This enabled the British army formations, now eight to twelve miles from Dunkirk, to move up on foot to the coast in the darkness of the storm. The violence of the rain with scarcely any interruption made it impossible for the Luftwaffe to operate in such turbulent conditions. Yet despite the storm in Flanders, a great calm, which has rarely been experienced before, settled over the English Channel during the days which followed, and its waters became as still as a mill pond.

It was this quite extraordinary and miraculous calm which enabled a vast armada of little ships, big ships, warships, privately owned motor-cruisers from British rivers and estuaries - in fact, almost anything that would float - to ply back and forth in a desperate bid to rescue as many of our men as possible

Douglas Bader, the legless Spitfire fighter ace, who flew with his squadrons from the fighter base at Martlesham, near Ipswich, to help cover the operation, described the scene in his book, Fight for the Sky:

> *The sea from Dunkirk to Dover during these days of the evacuation looked like any coastal road in England on a bank holiday. It was solid with shipping. One felt one could walk across without getting one's feet wet, or that's what it looked like from the air.*

There were naval escort vessels, sailing dinghies, rowing boats, paddle-steamers, indeed every floating device known in this country. They were all taking British soldiers from Dunkirk back home. You could identify Dunkirk from the Thames estuary by the huge pall of black smoke rising straight up into a windless sky from the oil tanks which were ablaze just inside the harbour.

Dunkirk Beaches, 1940
Picture Credit: Eurich, Richard Ernst (RA) Art.IWM ART LD 2277 Imperial War Museum (Public Domain)

To a very large extent, the German air squadrons were unable to intervene because so many of these squadrons still remained grounded. General Haider, Chief of the German General Staff, recorded in his diary on 30 May that 'Bad weather has grounded the Luftwaffe, and now we must stand by and watch countless thousands of the enemy getting away to England right under our noses.' And so it was. On the 4 June 1940, the Admiralty reported that the evacuation, codename "Operation Dynamo" had been completed. At the time Winston Churchill, having replaced Neville Chamberlain as Prime Minister on 10 May said it was "a miracle of deliverance." And it was.

As for my dad, having escaped from France, he found that 14 Fighter Group had ceased to exist for the time being having been disbanded in the chaos of the retreat from France. Dad therefore found himself among thousands of evacuees from the Air Component of the BEF and the AASF were being met at the quayside at Dover and other ports and directed to various military installations awaiting further orders.

As luck would have it, dad found himself back at RAF Uxbridge where he had done his basic training. It had become a transit and holding camp for BEF returnees. However, Dad did not remain at the RAF base for long. The RAF had other plans for him sooner than he had expected. He was off the the Channel Islands.

Chapter 3
THE CHANNEL ISLES

The Channel Islands are an archipelago in the English Channel, off the French coast of Normandy. They include two Crown dependencies: the Bailiwick of Jersey, which is the largest of the islands; and the Bailiwick of Guernsey, consisting of Guernsey, Alderney, Sark and some smaller islands. They are considered the remnants of the Duchy of Normandy and self-governing dependencies of the Crown. This means they have their own directly elected legislative assemblies, administrative, fiscal and legal systems and their own courts of law.

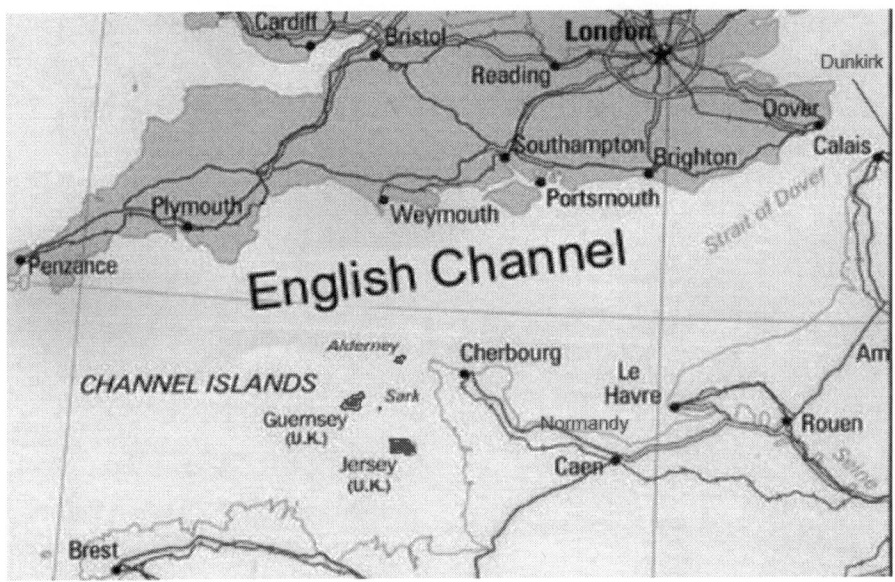

As Crown Dependencies Channel Islands are not represented in the UK Parliament but the UK has always been responsible for the defence and international relations of the islands.

Such was the case when Neville Chamberlain declared war on Germany on the 3 September 1939, and ushered in the period which became known as the Phoney war. This was an eight-month period at the start of World War II, during which there was only one limited military land operation on the Western Front, when French troops invaded Germany's Saar district.

During the Phoney war the Channel islanders carried on as normal including the horticulture and tourist trades. The new airport complex on Guernsey was put to good use for the tourist industry during this period even though it was taken over by RAF Coastal Command when war was declared. The new Guernsey Airport at La Villiaze, Forest, cost £100,500 to construct and had four grass runways, the longest was 1,000 yards. It offered night landing facilities, direction finding equipment and a concrete fog-line. The £14,000 state of the art two storey terminal building which housed the met office and air traffic control, as well as passenger handling facilities and earned the airport a reputation as one of the finest in the world at the time.

The Guernsey Airport terminal building taken which my dad helped to trash before the Germans could get their hands on the state of the art control systems
Picture Credit: Imperial War Museum (Public Domain, 1939)

The day after, the airport was officially opened on 5 May 1939, by the Air Minister Sir Kingsley Wood, Guernsey Airways and Jersey Airways (later Channel Island Airways) began operating passenger flights to Heston (London) and Southampton and weekend trips to Shoreham. These services carried 5,000 passengers before being reduced at the outbreak of war, when the RAF took over, but Channel Island Airways continued a limited service of flying the de Havilland Express, also known as the de Havilland DH86. This was a four-engined passenger aircraft manufactured by the de Havilland Aircraft Company between 1934 and 1937.

The British government relaxed restrictions on travel between the UK and the Channel Islands in March 1940, enabling tourists from the UK to take morale-boosting holidays in traditional island resorts. Little did dad know that he would be visiting the airport soon, but not as a holiday maker but to perform an important job on behalf of the RAF authorities. The Battle of France was reaching its climax on Empire Day, 24 May, when King George VI addressed his subjects by radio, saying:

> *The decisive struggle is now upon us ... Let no one be mistaken; it is not mere territorial conquest that our enemies are seeking. It is the overthrow, complete and final, of this Empire and of everything for which it stands, and after that the conquest of the world. And if their will prevails they will bring to its accomplishment all the hatred and cruelty which they have already displayed.*

On 11 June 1940, as part of the British war effort in the Battle of France, a long range RAF aerial sortie carried out by 36 Whitley bombers against the Italian cities of Turin and Genoa departed from the small airfields in Jersey and Guernsey, as part of Operation Haddock.

Weather conditions resulted in only 10 Whitleys reaching their intended targets. Two bombers were lost in the action. This was the only time when the Channel Islands were used directly in the war effort.

Events were now proceeding at a pace. As the German armed forces drove through France relentlessly towards the coast of the English Channel, it was clear to Churchill and the forces personnel who advised him, that the Channel Islands could not be defended. They served no strategic advantage and if the islanders resisted then the small towns and villages would be flattened by German bombers and there would be unacceptable casualties.

It was Churchill's intention to declare the Channel Islands, 'an open town', but the announcement was delayed in order for any military or other equipment which could be valuable to the enemy was salvaged or destroyed.

Guess who was to be part of the demilitarisation of the islands. That's right! My dad. As news reached his base in Uxbridge, that German forces had occupied Paris unopposed on the 14 June, dad found that he had been moved to RAF Henlow, Bedfordshire to await air transport. On the 16 June 1940 he boarded a de-Havilland Dominie biplane for the transit flight to Guernsey, at a time of great urgency.

On 17 June 1940, a plane arrived in Jersey from Bordeaux evacuating Brigade General Charles de Gaulle from France. After coffee and refuelling, the plane flew on to Heston, outside London, where next day the general made his historic appeal of 18 June to the French people via the BBC. This was the same day when the victorious German commanders met with French officials on 18 June to negotiate an end to hostilities.

On the Channel Islands, with no planning and secrecy being maintained, communications between the island governments and the UK took place in an atmosphere of confusion and misinterpretation. Opinion was divided, and chaos ensued with different policies adopted by the different islands. The British government concluded its best policy was to make available as many ships as possible so that islanders had the option to leave if they wanted to.

On 19 June the Guernsey local paper published announcements that plans were well in hand to evacuate all the children from the island, telling parents to go to their schools that evening to register and to prepare to send the children away the next day. Teachers were told they were expected to travel with their children bringing assistants to help, mothers volunteered. As many as 5,000 schoolchildren evacuated from Guernsey, while 1,000 stayed with 12 teachers. Amongst those who stayed were a number from the Castel school, who through a misunderstanding about the boat departure time, missed the sailing.

In Jersey, the situation was different. Children were on holiday to help with the potato crop, and the island authorities gave out mixed messages. They feared that what happened in France, would happen in Jersey. In France, ships had been mobbed, there were riots amongst travellers and in the empty towns, with looting of empty houses and shops.

The Island authorities decided to push the message that, 'staying was best', with posters saying "Don't be yellow, stay at home. Needless to say, with the British government advising islanders to evacuate as quickly as possible, this led to confusion and disorder. Consequently, there was no instruction to schools to evacuate. People could decide themselves if they or their children should evacuate.

On Jersey, only 1,000 evacuated with 67 teachers, many travelling with their parents, the remaining 4,500 remained with 140 teachers.

Throughout the islands, houses, cars and businesses were abandoned by those evacuating. Some locked their front doors, some did not, reasoning that someone would break the door to get in anyway. Some gave away pets, and others just released them, many put them down. Some gave away furniture and belongings, and some gave it to someone for safe storage, others simply walked away, leaving dirty dishes in the sink and food on the table. The withdrawal of cash from banks was limited to £20 per person. People could take just one suitcase. The Lieutenant Governor of Jersey and Lieutenant Governor of Guernsey left their islands on board ships on 21 June 1940, the day France surrendered.

In the last week of June, it was decided to demilitarise the islands and to evacuate a considerable part of the population. The Royal Guernsey Militia and the Jersey Militia were disbanded, and so, too, were the recently formed detachments of Local Defence Volunteers. The people were told that if they wished to leave for England they had only a few hours in which to pack, as boats were already waiting at the ports to take them across Channel.

An article in the weekly *The War Illustrated* magazine 19 July 1940 described the chaotic scene prior to the German occupation.

> *During the next few days, the customary placidity of the islands was rudely shattered. Houses which had been homes for generations were left in a shuttered abandonment. Potato and tomato fields were ploughed up, and though many of the great herds of Jersey and Guernsey cattle were shipped across the water, many, too, had to be destroyed.*

Motorcars driven to the ports were offered for sale at £1 apiece, but not a purchaser was forthcoming. Many a shopkeeper about to leave for England gave away his goods, and in the public-houses drinks were to be had for the asking. As there was no room on the boats for pets, the dogs and cats were shot, and so great was the run on the vet's services that the owners had to line up while their dumb friends were dispatched.

Of the total population of rather more than 90,000, some 25,000 sought safety in England. For the most part the refugees were young men of military age, women and children. They were evacuated by a motley collection of vessels, which included trawlers, potato boats and even a coal boat, and had to face a passage which even to Weymouth took twenty-four hours, and many of the vessels had only ship's biscuits and water on board.

For the majority of the islanders, however, the ties of home were too strong to be severed with such suddenness, and in their resolve to stay on were supported by the example of many of the leading members of their little communities.

The Jersey States of Parliament announced that, "we were remaining at our posts to carry on our duties, and we are all of us keeping with us in these islands our wives and families."

In Guernsey, the King's Procurer told his people that he would inform the Nazis when they came that the Islanders had no arms and would offer no resistance, and would ask that their enforced submission should not be abused; and Mrs. Hathaway, Dame of Sark, similarly intimated that she was remaining in her diminutive domain.

While all this mayhem was going on my dad was busy at the Guernsey Airport at La Villiaze assisting in the recovery of valuable signal equipment. Items that could not be recovered were destroyed. Dad and other RAF personnel systematically sabotaged the airport's modern aeronautical technology to make it unserviceable to the enemy. This included the state of the art instrumentation of the air traffic control systems in the terminal building, which they destroyed beyond repair. The Germans were not going to have access to that equipment, my dad and his colleagues made sure of that.

Dad was only on Guernsey for a few days, and having completed his assignment, he was flown back to England. His flight probably took place on the 26 June and was done in the nick of time. The Germans did not realise that the islands had been demilitarised and were "open towns." They expected to fight for the islands, and the Wehrmacht was preparing Operation Grunpfeil (Green Arrow), a planned invasion of the islands with assault troops comprising two battalions.

On 28 June 1940, the Germans began their assault by sending a squadron of bombers over the islands and bombed the harbours of Guernsey and Jersey. In St. Peter Port, the main town of Guernsey, some lorries lined up to load tomatoes for export to England were mistaken by the reconnaissance flights for troop carriers.

The Luftwaffe's bombing of Weighbridge, St. Peter Port, Guernsey, on 28 June 1940
Picture Credit: Film Inspector (Public Domain)

A similar attack occurred in Jersey where nine died. In total, 44 islanders were killed in the raids. The BBC broadcast a belated message that the islands had been declared "open towns" and later in the day reported the German bombing of the island.

Checking this out, a reconnaissance pilot, Hauptmann Liebe-Pieteritz, made a test landing at Guernsey's deserted airfield at La Villiaze on 30 June to determine the level of defence. He reported his brief landing to Luftflotte 3 which came to the decision that the islands were not defended. As a result, a platoon of Luftwaffe airmen was flown that evening to Guernsey by Junkers transport planes. Inspector Sculpher of the Guernsey police went to the airport carrying a letter signed by the bailiff stating that,"This Island has been declared an Open Island by His Majesty's Government of the United Kingdom. There are no armed forces of any description. The bearer has been instructed to hand this communication to you. He does not understand the German language.

Inspector Sculpher found that the airport had been taken over by the Luftwaffe. The senior German officer, Major Albrecht Lanz, asked to be taken to the island's chief man. They went by police car to the Royal Hotel where they were joined by the bailiff, the president of the controlling committee, and other officials. Lanz announced through an interpreter that Guernsey was now under German occupation. In this way the Luftwaffe pre-empted the Wehrmacht's invasion plans.

Jersey surrendered on 1 July. Alderney, where only a handful of islanders remained, was occupied on 2 July and a small detachment travelled from Guernsey to Sark, which surrendered on 4 July. The first shipborne German troops consisting of two anti-aircraft units, arrived in St. Peter Port on the captured freighter SS Holland on 14 July.

In subsequent months Luftwaffe Junkers 52 troop carriers, Dornier DO 17 bombers, Heinkel He 111 bombers, Henschel Hs 126 reconnaissance aircraft, ME109 fighters and Junkers Ju 87 dive bombers established themselves on the Jersey and Guernsey former tourist airbases from where they flew to attack England during the Battle of Britain.

The occupation of the Channel Islands had now begun, and the islanders would not be liberated until on 9 May 1945, when the war with Germany came to an end.

As a postscript, British Liberation forces arrived in the islands on 12 May 1945. A Royal Proclamation read out by Brigadier Alfred Snow in both Guernsey and Jersey vested the authority of military government in him. The British Government had planned for the relief and restoration of order in the islands. Food, clothing, pots, pans and household necessities had been stockpiled so as to supply islanders immediately.

It was decided that to minimise financial disruption Reichsmarks would continue in circulation until they could be exchanged for sterling.

In Sark, Mary Hathaway DBE (1884-1974) who was the feudal ruler of the island most of her life, ruling for 47 years, was left in command of the 275 German troops in the island until 17 May when they were transferred as prisoners of war to England.

The UK Home Secretary, Herbert Morrison, visited Guernsey on 14 May and Jersey on 15 May and offered an explanation in person to the States in both bailiwicks as to why it had been felt in the interests of the islands not to defend them in 1940 and not to use force to liberate them after D-Day. Finally, on 7 June the King and Queen visited Jersey and Guernsey to welcome the oldest possessions of the Crown back to freedom.

The old terminal building prior to its demolition in May 2004
Picture Credit: Guernsey Airport Authority, (Public Domain)

The old terminal building was demolished in May 2004 and the spoil from the demolition was used in the foundations of a new aircraft apron. The new terminal handled more than 900,000 passengers during 2005, but has capacity for up to 1.25 million a year.

Continuing with my dad's story, upon returning from Guernsey, he was immediately posted to a new unfinished bomber station at RAF Oakington, 6 miles northwest of Cambridge. With an invasion of England to be expected, along with anyone else, who could handle a weapon, dad was inducted into the important role of ground defence needed for the air defence of Britain.

Chapter 4
PUSHED FROM PILLAR TO POST

As July 1940 opened Great Britain embarked on a battle for which there was no precedent in the annals of warfare. The fate of the nation and the Empire depended entirely on the outcome of a strategic conflict in the sky which became known to the annals of history as The Battle of Britain. The whole country was on invasion alert because should the Luftwaffe gain air superiority there would be nothing to stop Hitler ordering the commencement of "Operation Sea Lion", the invasion of Great Britain.

RAF Oakington, Cambridgeshire (July 1940)

After returning from the Channel Islands, dad was posted to a bomber station at RAF Oakington, Cambridgeshire, in July 1940, which was still under construction. When dad arrived at the airbase, it had become home to No. 218 Squadron which had recently returned from France. The squadron was equipped with a single-engine light bomber called the Fairey Battle.

Three Fairey Battle fighter bombers of No 218 Squadron over France (1940)
Picture Credit: Imperial War Museum (Public Domain)

The Fairey Battle bomber had a three-man crew and bomb load. Although a great improvement over bombers that preceded it, this bomber was relatively slow and limited in range. With only two Browning .303 machine guns as defensive armament, it was found to be highly vulnerable to enemy fighters and anti-aircraft fire in France.

Equipped with the Fairey Battle bomber the squadron suffered heavy losses, and the unit was hastily evacuated to RAF Oakington, where it was re-equipped with the two engined Bristol Blenheim.

The Blenheim was one of the first British aircraft at the time which was constructed with an all-metal stressed-skin, retractable landing gear, flaps, a powered gun turret and variable-pitch propellers. However, it was not much better than its predecessor. So when 50 Blenheims supported the Dunkirk evacuation by harassing enemy forces it was vulnerable to the fast German monoplanes like the Messerschmitt BF 109 and suffered heavy losses.

Bristol Blenheim Mk IV L4842 being flown by test pilot Bill Pegg near Filton, 29 May 1939
Picture Credit: Imperial War Museum (Public Domain)

By June 1940, daylight Blenheim losses were so high that Fighter Command decided that the plane should be relegated mainly to night fighter duties where No. 23 Squadron RAF, which had already operated the type under nighttime conditions, had better success. The Blenheim proved to be an invaluable night fighter.

Surrounded by Blenheim and Fairey Battle bombers at RAF Oakington, there was one memorable event occurred at RAF Oakington on the 19 September 1940, which dad witnessed. Blenheim bombers from 218 squadron also based at Oakington, were making mock attacks on the airfield for the benefit of the army and RAF defenders.

Suddenly a Luftwaffe Junkers Ju88a appeared, obviously in trouble, and made a crash landing on the airfield. Lieutenant Helmut Knab and his crew were detained. It turned out that German aircraft was involved in photo reconnaissance and it yielded valuable equipment.

The excellent cameras were soon put to good use when on the 16 November 1940 No. 3 Photo-Reconnaissance Unit formed at Oakington tasked with damage assessment duties over Germany.

Dad commenced a two-week Ground Gunnery course, held at the station, on 1st October 1941. He said:

> *The next destination for us was a place called Oakington, which was about seven miles outside of Cambridge, where I was given tuition in ground defence. This included learning the art of firing guns etc and where we were to be based for the next few months.*

RAF Ground Defence Gunners manning a Browning 303 machine gun like my dad did
Picture Credit: Imperial War Museum (Public Domain)

Upon the completion of his training dad was qualified as Ground Defence Gunner and assigned to the stations anti-aircraft defences manning a Browning 303 machine gun. His character and trade assessment as recorded on New Years Eve 1940 was "Very Good."

At first, dad's duties were not so bad and consisted of shift work, two hours on then off alternately for twenty-four hours, followed by twenty-four hours off duty. However, dad's living conditions were crude to say the least. He told my mother:

> *We slept under canvass during summer, duties consisted of shift work, two hours on then off alternately for twenty four hours, followed by twenty four hours off duty, but all too soon the snow came! This was followed by a freezing cold winter 1941-1942, we were still at this time at nights under canvass.*

There must have been a foot of snow outside each tent, however around about this time, I had leave due to me. I took ten days leave and went up to Leek in Staffordshire to visit my mother who along with others had been evacuated from the coast-lines. She was staying with her sister who owned a pub there, so it was to be for me a very welcome respite.

No sooner had dad returned to RAF Oakington, his new position as a Gunner put him into a different trade group and he was promoted to Leading Aircraftman (LAC) on the 1 February 1941 with the substantial pay rise to 5 shillings (25 pence) per day! That was a pleasant surprise, but the RAF do not do things without a reason. Within weeks dad was posted to RAF Syreston, 6 miles south-west of Newark-on-Trent, Nottinghamshire.

RAF Syreston, Nottinghamshire (March 1941)

RAF Syrestonn had opened on 1 December 1940 as an operational bomber station in No. 1 Group, Bomber Command. Dad was assigned to airfield ground defence duties. This was during the period when the airbase was closed until 5 May 1942, whilst a concrete runway was built with two T2 hangars.

When it re-opened, it became part of No. 5 Group. Meanwhile, dad's expertise as a Ground Defence Gunner and the way he helped new recruits in the use the anti-aircraft guns at the base did not escape the notice of his superiors. He was soon selected for training as a gunnery instructor and posted to the Isle of Man for training.

RAF Ronaldsway, Isle of Man (4 June 1941)

Situated in the middle of the Irish Sea, the Isle of Man has a long association with aviation. The airfield at Ronaldsway can trace its origins back to 1929 when Sir Alan Cobham's' Air Circus flew from a large field close to the village.

Later in 1934, Blackpool and West Coast Air Services acquired the land and thus started the nucleolus of a proper airport. At the beginning of December 1939 No. 1 Ground Defence Gunners School was established and under the control of Technical Training Command its role was to train Airmen for ground defence duties.

Dad arrived at RAF Ronaldsway on 4 June 1941 to commence a 4-week Gunnery Instructors Course. On the same day he completed the course (1 July) dad was promoted to the rank of corporal. In that capacity dad received a daily pay of 5 shillings and 6 pence (27.5 pence), a welcome pay rise. This is about £11 in today's money. Within a month, dad had received orders to report to RAF Balderton, situated 2 miles south of Newark-on Trent, to put his training into practice. Once again dad was back in Cambridgeshire.

RAF Balderton, Cambridgeshire (11 August 1941)

Dad arrived at RAF Balderton on the 11 August 1941 and was immediately assigned to ground defence duties but with the additional responsibilities of supervising the training of new gunners. The base proved to be a popular move for dad and his friends, as it provided a bit of entertainment and night life for all the off-duty periods. There was even a four piece band at the local hop.

Things were about to change and in the middle of November, the airbase was passed to the control of No. 5 Group Bomber Command and was now a satellite airfield to Syreston. As a consequence, on the 24 November 1941 dad received orders to join 61 Operational Training Unit (OTU) at RAF Rednal in Shropshire for ground defence duties.

RAF Rednal, Shropshire (25 November 1941)

When dad arrived at RAF Rednal, he was surprised to find that he was the first Airman to arrive as it appeared there was a new aerodrome in the process of being built.

The only other occupant there from the services was a retired Army Major, who had been brought out of retirement to help organise the ground defence at this particular aerodrome.

RAF Rednal was never designed for combat as it was situated far from the east coast, but it had some defensive features such as bunkers, machine gun nests and an underground 2-room battlefield headquarters. Its main function was to train pilots to fly the iconic Spitfire. The remote location made it safe from enemy bombardment and a good place to send foreign pilots for training in case they were not entirely to be trusted.

Rednal was to produce some of the finest air-aces of the era - pilots like Buerling, Wojda, Clostermann and hosts of others, many tragically killed, they would arrive at Rednal, sometimes having escaped from occupied continental Europe, get trained up and be sent on to places like Biggin Hill. But that was the future and dad was concerned with the now.

Dad was fed up. He had been moved from pillar to post and despite all of the training he had undergone/done, he had ended up in the middle of nowhere, on a construction site for a new airbase that was far removed from the war.

Dad felt deflated and isolated as he gazed upon the building workers, who were constructing runways and assembling hangers for housing the aircraft. To make matters worse, the nearest town was eight miles away, a place called Oswestry, which was near the Welsh border and there was no service bus.

A week later after dad's arrival at the construction site, dad was joined by other RAF personnel, cooks, ground crews and transport staff and things brightened up, but by now dad had come to the conclusion that this was not the life for him. He envisaged that it would be more of the same. He'd had his fill of ground duties.

With little thought for the future consequences of his actions, dad requested an interview with his Commanding Officer to discuss his situation. Mum wrote in her notes what dad dictated to her about what happened next, and you can detect in his words the frustrations that he felt.

> *I soon realised that this was not the life for me, I'd had my fill of ground duties, along with so much what seemed at times like unnecessary discipline. So! To get out of this boring situation, what was to be done? Without more ado and I must admit without much thought, I decided to volunteer for Air-crew.*

Volunteering for aircrew duties was a decision that would one day haunt him for the rest of his life, but for now he felt elated that he would escape from the tedium and boredom which had been his lot up to that time. So in the spring of 1942, dad found himself on a train bound for London and the Aircrew Assessment Centre at St Johns Wood.

> *After an interview with my C.O. who by this time had arrived at the aerodrome, I went up to St Johns Wood in London in front of a selection board to undergo various medical tests. I had eye tests etc plus intelligence tests. Upon passing each of these examinations, I was then sent to Shrewsbury Aerodrome.*
>
> *After just a few weeks at Shrewbury unfortunately, I contracted pneumonia, so was in hospital for five weeks, followed by two weeks in Wellington convalescent home Shropshire. Following my recovery and soon after my arrival back at camp, confirmation came through - my application for Aircrew had been accepted!*

Little did dad know at the time what he was getting himself into or what it was that he would end up doing. All he knew was that he had escaped from what he thought was endless boredom and that he would be a member of a flight crew in a bomber. That sounded exciting.

Chapter 5
AIR GUNNER SERGEANT HAYWARD

If dad thought that he would no longer be pushed from pillar to post he was very much mistaken. All service aircrew, irrespective of the role into which they would eventually serve, had to undergo a period of training at an Initial Training Wing (ITW). Dad reported to 15 ITW at RAF Bridlington on the 5 September 1942 to commence the mandatory eight week training course.

RAF Bridlington, Yorkshire (5 September 1942)

Wearing the distinctive white shoulder flashes of an Aircrew Cadet dad retained his substantive rank of Corporal. However, this rank would carry no authority throughout his period of basic training at 15 ITW. Here all recruits were treated as though they were new entrants to the service as indeed as many of his contemporaries would have been.

> *On the move again, to initial training wing in Bridlington, Yorkshire for about six weeks complete with white flash on hat to denote Air-crew training cadet, but still retaining the rank of Corporal at the same time!*

According to official records, the making of a fighting airman requires physical fitness and discipline. Day after day the recruits drilled, marched and attended lectures. The intensive course was designed not only to build comradeship and pride but also to weed out those who would not accept the strict discipline required of flying operations.

It would have been a strenuous time, in which muscle, nerve and brain would have been toned to perfection. The syllabus of training at these units, intensive though it was, was carefully balanced so that while the embryo airman retained his enthusiasm and individuality, he acquired a sense of discipline and developed a team spirit. Individuality is a necessary quality for aerial fighting, but there had to be discipline and "crew spirit."

RAF Bridlington was not an airfield but had more of the appearance of an army camp. This absence of an airfield and aircraft was of course deliberate as it removed all distraction and focused the minds of the prospective aircrew recruits on their ultimate goal of attaining aircrew status. Training was therefore very intense.

Proper service conduct protocols was learned with drilling, saluting and RAF Administration being taught. This together with physical training, morse-code learning and aircraft recognition, coupled with lectures on mathematics, science, weaponry, anti-gas measures and navigation was all part of the discipline needed to ensure that each crew member knew what their role in the Stirling aircraft would be. There could be no room for error.

Dad completed his training and passed out from 15 ITW on Friday, 30 October 1942 and was granted 7 days leave, for which he was issued with a travel warrant to his home and onward documentation to his next posting which was RAF Llandwrog in North Wales.

RAF Llandwrog, Wales (Mid-November 1942)

Llandwrog airfield was built on a peninsula jutting out into Caernarfon Bay. It opened in January 1941 and will forever have a place in the history of the RAF because it was here that the RAF Mountain Rescue Service came into being.

Before the war the local police, with the aid of civilian volunteers, dealt with the infrequent crashes in the hills of Wales. This arrangement proved totally inadequate once wartime training moved to the area.

In the five months from July to December 1942 there were ten major accidents in the hills of North Wales resulting in 40 fatalities and 8 injured. The need for a dedicated Mountain Rescue Service was all too obvious and so it came into being in February 1943. It remains an important part of the Royal Air Forces organisation to this day.

Llandwrog had opened as a base for No. 9 Air Gunnery School (AGS) and served as a satellite airfield to Penrhos, some 20 miles away near Pwellheli. Built on a low-lying peninsula it was subject to frequent flooding and operations were often confined to Penrhos. In June 1942 No. 9 Air Gunnery School was renamed No. 9 (Observers) Advanced Flying Unit. (OAFU). This name change did not alter the primary function of Penrhos and Llandwrog, which was the training of air gunners for Bomber Command. Training was conducted in a variety of aircraft including Avro Anson's, Armstrong Whitworth Whitley's and Bristol Blenheims.

Dad arrived at Llandwrog in the middle of November 1942 where he began the inevitable ground school phase of his air gunnery course. In the classroom he was taught the mechanics and workings of the hydraulically operated gun turret and the Browning machine gun with which the majority of RAF bombers were equipped.

The principles of "gun laying" where the gunner had to allow for the relative movement of the intended target and the effects of speed, wind, and the other myriad of events that conspire to make airborne gunnery a difficult skill to acquire.

Interestingly by the time dad had arrived at 9 OAFU the RAF had introduced a gunnery training simulator. This "simulator" basically consisted of projecting the image of a moving target on to a large screen housed within a purpose, built building. The trainee manoeuvred his guns that projected a cross onto the moving target indicating where his "shots" had hit. Several of these buildings still exist round the country and in Shropshire one is now in use as an office block.

By the time that dad's course was due to commence the flying phase of their training Llandwrog airfield had succumbed to the vagaries of the Welsh winter and its runways, which were actually some several feet below sea level, had become waterlogged. A move to Penrhos just prior to Christmas 1942 allowed the flying phase of the course to commence. This was something that dad enjoyed.

RAF Penrhos, Wales (December 1942)

Gunnery School RAF Penrhos
Picture Credit: Imperial War Museum (Public Domain)

Dad, like all trainees, manned the mid upper gun turret of a Bristol Blenheim and he conducted numerous sorties over the Irish Sea where initially he would fire at targets on the surface of the water before progressing to live firing at sleeve targets towed by other aircraft. At the end of the sortie, both aircraft would return to Penrhos where he could inspect the canvas sleeve and note how many hits he had registered.

> *My next move was to Llandwrog in Wales near Caernarfon, but this was a short lived stay because after there being continual rain for two weeks, the airdrome was completely flooded, especially the runways and we were situated on the coast-line, apparently below sea level at high tide. Consequently, our only option was to move on to Penrhos for six weeks, and it was here that I had first hand experience in firing guns from the turrets of a Blenheim flying at low level above the sea.*
>
> *This was ground to sea exercise or air to air firing, which was turret to drogue, drogue meaning "canvass sleeve", which was towed behind another aircraft.*

It was on one of these trainee flights that dad came to believe he had a Guardian Angel. On the 19 February 1943 he was detailed to fly on one of his final training sorties in the mid upper gun turret of a Blenheim. Answering a late call of nature dad returned to the crew ready room to find that his flight had been called early and another trainee had taken his place. The Blenheim bomber took off from Penros but hardly had it got airborne, it almost immediately suffered an engine failure. The pilot was unable to control the struggling aircraft and it stalled and crashed into high ground approximately half a mile west of the airfield. The aircraft was consumed by fire and all the crew of five perished.

One particular day after being detailed for one of these flights, I had a sudden call of nature and on my return discovered that my flight had been called and had already left the building with another trainee taking my place.

Unfortunately, this aircraft crashed into a field about five miles from the base, sadly everyone on board was killed. Apparently one of the engines had failed.

I thought then that I had a Guardian Angel! This was not to be the last time that I believed this to be so!

Dad completed his training on the 26 March 1943 and as was customary he was awarded his Observers Brevet.

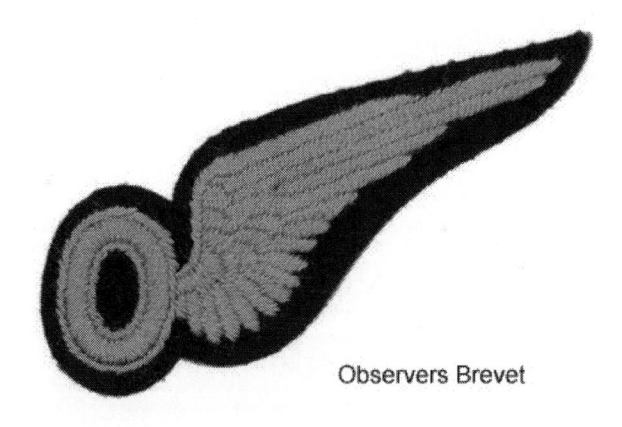

Observers Brevet

What now? The suggestion was put forward that dad remain at Penrhos as an instructor, this no doubt being influenced by his attendance at the Ground Defence Gunners School at Ronaldsway where he had passed out as an instructor. However, dad declined this offer.

After completing my training as an air gunner, I was requested to stay on as an instructor having had previous experience in instructing on "Browning" machine guns which were also used in aircraft, but declined this offer (though was to regret this decision many times later) as I felt the need at the time for more operational experience so on becoming a fully fledged air-gunner, was now promoted from Corporal to Sergeant and then posted to a place called Water-Beach not far from Cambridge.

Dad having qualified as a fully fledged air-gunner received the Air-Gunner Brevet. He was promoted from Corporal to Sergeant and got a pay rise. This was 9 shillings and 6 pence (47.5 pence) per day, about £21.50 in today's money. He was then posted to RAF Waterbeach not far from Cambridge. He really looked the business in his uniform marked with the coveted Air-Gunner Brevet.

Chapter 6
DAD GOES A GARDENING

There was no leave after the intensive gunnery course in Wales. Bomber Command was intensifying their operations against Germany, and replacement crews were urgently needed by the operational squadrons, even though some may be new and inexperienced. So it was that on 27 March 1943 dad received orders to report to No.1651 Heavy Conversion Unit (HCU) at RAF Waterbeach, which is about 5.5 miles north of Cambridge.

As dad made his way to RAF Waterbeach by train, he was interrupted along the way by an unexpected, but welcome break.

> *Our train only went as far as Crewe along with another two airmen. We made our way from the station to look for a night lodge somewhere and lo and behold, there was this inn, just a few steps up the road. Unfortunately, there were no rooms available, however, a customer kindly offered to accommodate us, he and his wife gave up their bed for the three of us to share, they were also having a party that night, it was somebody's birthday apparently. We fell in for a very good night and it was very much appreciated, especially as in the morning before we left, this good couple cooked us a fine breakfast of eggs bacon, fresh tomatoes and fried bread, certainly a luxurious breakfast in those days - they must of given up their whole weeks rations for us.*

RAF Waterbeach, Cambridgeshire (29 March 1943)

Dad finally reached RAF Waterbeach and here he was teamed up with other aircrew, pilots, navigators, bomb aimers, etc. and they would be brought together to form a crew destined to fly the Short Stirling, a four-engined bomber which carried a crew of seven.

A Short Stirling of No. 1651 being refuelled at Waterbeach, 1942.
Picture Credit: photograph HU 107753, Imperial War Museums (Public Domain)

The Stirling was a heavy bomber manufactured by Short Brothers in Rochester and Belfast and in the first years of the Second World War formed the core of the British RAF heavy bomber units that took the war to Germany. During its use as a bomber, pilots praised the type for its ability to out-turn enemy night fighters and its favourable handling characteristics. Due to the thick wing, the Stirling could out-turn the JU 88 and BF 110 night fighters they faced. Its handling was much better than that of the Halifax and some preferred it to the Lancaster.

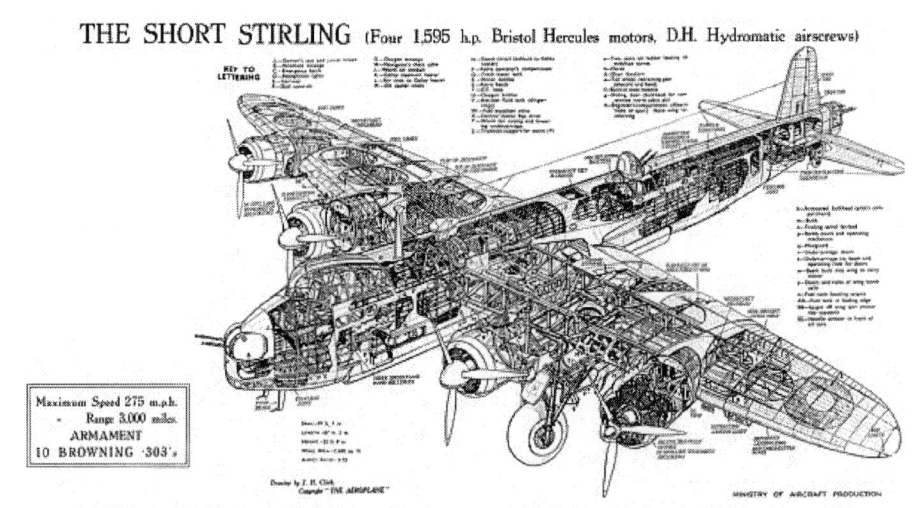

Picture Credit: This work created by the United Kingdom Government is in the public domain.
https://commons.wikimedia.org/wiki/File:Short_Stirling_bomber_cutaway_drawing_circa_1943_(44266122).png

The Stirling did have an Achilles heel, though. It had disappointing performance at maximum altitude as a consequence of the thick wing. Even so, based on its flight characteristics, Flight Lieutenant Peden (RCAF) of No. 214 Squadron RAF described the Stirling as "one of the finest aircraft ever built."

The first few Short Stirling MK Is were powered by 4 Bristol Hercules XI radial piston engines. But most of the later productions were powered with 1,500 HP Hercules XI engines. They had a speed of 255 mph. The Stirling MK III had a speed of 270 mph owing to its four 1,635 HP Hercules VI engines, which was different from that of its predecessors.

The Stirling's 14000 lb bomb load was double that of any other bomber flying from the British-based aviation firm. It had a crew of seven, with a 4000-mile range at its standard speed, along with a 10,000 pounds weapons load over 2300 miles. Its armament comprised of 2 x 7.7mm machine guns in the powered nose-turret, upper-turret and rear-turret.

Dad arrived at RAF Waterbeach on 29 March 1943 after a two-day journey and almost immediately commenced his 6 week training course together with other aircrew that would form the seven men Stirling bomber crew in which he would be a member.

During the course dad's aircrew honed their combined skills until they became a cohesive team to carry out the deadly and hazardous task of taking the war to Germany. It was the custom that they would continue to fly together for the whole of their assigned tour of duty. Dad was assigned to the mid-upper gun position in the aircraft.

Dad completed the course on 7 May 1943 whereupon the newly formed crew were posted to 149 Squadron based at Lakenheath, Suffolk.

Lakenheath Aerodrome, Suffolk (9 May 1943)

> *After this course was completed, we were sent to Lakenheath Aerodrome in Suffolk for operational service. Our crew consisted of seven including myself.*

The pilot was called Jack, though I cannot recall his surname; he was a jovial happy person given to playing pranks and telling jokes! I remember his hair was blond and curly. We all considered him to be a fine skipper.

Nigel was our navigator, a more retiring type of person, but very likeable. The rear gunner Bill was a Scotsman, and the engineer who's name I also cannot recall though can picture his face so clearly was the shortest member of the crew, he was also fair haired and happy go- lucky. The person known as the bomb aimer was also the second pilot, and he was trained to take over from the skipper in emergencies, he was required when necessary to act as front gunner.

Our wireless operator was a Canadian and like myself just an ordinary type of chap. They were a good bunch and we mixed well with each other, plus we were roughly the same age, all in our early twenties.

Under the command of Petty Officer Jack Sutherst, the pilot, the fresh crew arrived at RAF Lakenheath on the 9 May 1943. The following morning they reported to the Squadron Adjutant who introduced them to their Squadron Commanding Officer, Wing Commander G E Harrison DFC (Distinguished Flying Cross).

Over the next two weeks, dad and his fellow crewmen flew an intensive period of training flights. This involved conducting a series of short and long range navigation exercises, some to the north of Scotland.

Practise bombing runs were also conducted and fighter affiliation exercises carried out. The gunners would have been allowed to do some live firing over the Irish Sea. Initially these training exercises would have been carried out in daylight but latterly all training would have been conducted at night because at this stage of the war Bomber Command operations were conducted almost exclusively at night.

On 28 May 1943, Wing Commander Harrison flew with the crew on a simulated bombing mission to evaluate their competence. Having proved themselves worthy they were declared operational and the following night they flew their first operational sortie.

The crew as recorded by official RAF records

Rank	Service No.	Name	Crew Position
P/Off	156620	Jack Sutherst	Pilot
		Nigel	Navigator
Sgt	1207018	Arthur Harris	Wireless Operator/Air Gunner
Sgt	1109844	Ronald Harry Nash	Flight Engineer
Sgt	1387091	Eric Nigel Nicholson Beldon	Bomb Aimer
Sgt.	635625	Harold Sidney Hayward	Air Gunner Mid Upper Turret
Sgt.		William N Kinsey	Air Gunner Rear Turret

(1- 6 June, "Gardening" over in the waters around the Frisian Islands)

It was normal for the first operational sortie of a new crew to be of a fairly low key. Known in the RAF as "milk runs" because they were perceived to be of relatively low risk they were, nevertheless, an important part of Bomber Commands operations.

Codenamed "Gardening" the importance of sowing mines to disrupt enemy shipping demanded a continuous effort by the crews of Bomber Command throughout the war.

Between 1 to 2 June 1943 dad and his fellow crew members was tasked with "Gardening" the waters round the Frisian Islands, a chain of islands off the west coast of Denmark and Holland.

> *Our first operation consisted of laying mines off the Dutch coast in the hope that German ships would get involved with them, our crew completed three of these mining trips.*

The three "Gardening" sorties flown by dad and the crew were conducted during a lull in the main bomber offensive. There had been no major raids carried out by Bomber Command since the night of 29 May when the bombers had bombed Wuppertal, a city in North Rhine-Westphalia, Germany, in and around the Wupper valley, east of Düsseldorf and south of the Ruhr. On that night 611 heavy bombers of the Royal Air Force dropped close to 300,000 incendiary bombs and 60 4,000lb heavy explosives here. They raised the first firestorm of the second world war: 2,500 people were killed and the streets burned; 90% of the town was destroyed.

The reason for the break of bomber operations by Bomber Command at this time was due to the phase of the moon. A full moon made night operations all the more hazardous. However, it would not long before dad would experience his baptism of fire over the industrial areas of the Ruhr, and the cities of Duseldoff and Cologne.

Chapter 7
BAPTISM OF FIRE

The Battle of the Ruhr of 1943 was a 5-month British campaign of strategic bombing between 5 March 1943 - 31 July 1943 against the Nazi Germany Ruhr Valley, which had coke plants, steelworks, and 10 synthetic oil plants. To all air crew who flew in 1943 this was one target that made their stomach muscles tighten. They called it the "land of no return", and for good reason. To someone who did not fly in that period it is best described as the air battle of the Somme or Passchendaele, in which the bombers and their crews went out time and time again similar to the soldier who, in World War I went over the top time after time.

As soon as the coast was crossed, it was a case of running the gauntlet to the target and back, through enemy searchlights, heavy and light flack and fighter aircraft. The mental strain of continually having to key themselves up to face this, contrasting with rest days or aborted operations when they could unwind, relax and try and forget that war, was considerable. The effect was rather like a coiled spring continually being wound, run down and then wound up again.

There were also times when having got to the perimeter of the airfield and ready to take off, a signal to abort the operation would be received. This often induced a feeling of anticlimax among the aircrew. Until a crew had completed the thirty operations, there would be no respite and no choice but to get on with it.

It was during the Battle of the Ruhr, that a special operation during the night of May 16/17, 1943, that became famous. This was when Bomber Command carried out an attack on the reservoirs in the Sauerland in the Dambuster raid under the dubious name of "Operation Chastise." Its main targets were the dams of the Möhne, Sorpe, Eder, Lister and Ennepe. In the course of this violent mission, the important Möhne and Eder dams were destroyed and the resultant gigantic flood in the Ruhr valley killed about 2,000 people. More than 70 people were also killed when the Eder dam was blown up.

The Battle of the Ruhr had been going for three months, and 149 squadron's Stirlings had already been involved in raids over Essen, Mulheim, Duisburg, Dortmund and Bochum. Now it was time for dad's Stirling and crew to join the fray, and their first mission could not have been more worse. Their baptism of fire was to be a bombing raid on one of the largest and most heavily defended cities in the Ruhr.

Duseldoff in the Ruhr Valley (11/12 June 1943)

On 11/12 June 1943 dad found himself among 783 aircraft en route to Duseldoff, a city which lies in the centre of both the Rhine-Ruhr and the Rhineland Metropolitan Regions with the Cologne Bonn Region to its south and the Ruhr to its north. Zero hour had been set for 01.20 hrs, and 13 Pathfinder Oboe equipped Mosquito's led the way.

Oboe was a British aerial blind bombing navigation system based on radio transponder technology. The system consisted of a pair of radio transmitters at well-separated locations in England to transmit a signal to a Mosquito Pathfinder bomber carrying a radio transponder. The transponder re-transmitted the signals, which were then received by the two stations. The round-trip time of each signal gave the distance to the bomber.

Each Oboe station used radio ranging to define a circle of specific radii, with the intersection of the two circles pinpointing the target. The Mosquito flew along the circumference of the circle defined by one station, known as the "Cat", and dropped its load (either bombs or marking flares, depending on the mission) when it reached the intersection with the circle defined by another station, known as "Mouse." Oboe was used extensively by Pathfinder marker aircraft during the Battle of the Ruhr in 1943.

On route to Duseldoff there was almost total cloud cover with icing but over the target the weather conditions were good. The Pathfinder marking was good apart from one Mosquito, which released its load of Tl's (Target Indicators) 14 miles north east of Dusseldorf. This resulted in some of the main force dropping its bomb load over open country. However, the main bombing caused extensive damage to the centre of Dusseldorf.

In the raid some 64 factories were damaged, including tool and heavy armaments factories. Another factory that was making torpedoes and parts for U Boats was also badly damaged.

In all 2000 tons of bombs were dropped and 1500 acres of the city and main industrial area were demolished. German reports state that there were 8,882 separate fires of which 1,444 were classified as large. The gas supplies to the city were disrupted for 17 days and the water sewerage systems seriously damaged. 30,000 dwelling units were destroyed and a further 20,000 damaged rendering 140,000 people homeless. The dock area was badly hit with eight ships sunk or badly damaged. The known death toll was 1,292 with many more missing.

One can only imagine the frightening experience that my dad and his fellow crew members must have suffered during their first night bombing sorte. German defences were very active that night and in the Dusseldorf and Oberhausen areas the flack was so intensive that towards the end of the raid it was an almost continuous barrage. There were many searchlights in operation and these periodically focused upon individual bombers so that one of the 73 ground-controlled enemy night-fighters that engaged the bomber force could easily target their prey.

Dad no doubt made use of his guns in the upper-gun turret but even so, it would have been a terrifying experience to fire on the deadly shadows of German night fighters which dogged the bomber formation. A German report stated, "British bombers flew over West German territory, in particular the town of Oberhausen. 21 bombers were shot down." In fact the final figure was 38 aircraft were lost. Aircrew casualties were 153 killed and 25 parachuted to safety to become prisoners of war.

After his first raid over Duseldoff dad had survived his baptism of fire and I have no doubt he was relieved when his next mission, on 14/15 June 1943 was mine laying off the Brittany Coast and the River Gironde. It gave him and his fellow crew mates the opportunity to reassess their situation although of course, for dad, the die was cast and he could do nothing about it. If he thought that mine laying was an easy option, he was to be mistaken.

Although only 29 Stirlings took part in the operation, a Stirling from 75 Squadron was shot down. "Gardening" had become a dangerous pastime.

Breuil Steelworks at Le Creusot, France (19/20 June 1943)

On the 19/20 June dad's Sterling took part in a bombing raid on the Schneider Armaments Factory and the Breuil Steelworks at Le Creusot, France. This was an important target. It was not to be part of the main offensive against Germany but was one of those raids designed to keep the Germans guessing as to where the next target would be.

The official account of the raid of 290 aircraft was made up of 2 Lancasters, 181 Halifax and 107 Stirling bombers. This was still a large force for German defence to worry about, especially when they did not know what the target was. The tactics of the raid were that Stirling Pathfinders would only drop flares and that each crew of the Main Force was to identify their part of the target by the light of these flares.

The Main Force was to make two runs over the target area. Lingering smoke and the fact that crews were used to bombing on Target Indicators (Tl's) made visual identification difficult. Later photographs revealed that all crews had bombed within 3 miles of the centre of the target but only about a fifth of the bombs hit the factories. Many bombs fell on nearby residential areas, but no reports of casualties were made available. Two bombers were shot down.

Krefeld in the Ruhr Valley (21/22 June 1943)

Dad's next bomber sortie was the next day during the night of 21/22 June, once again in the heart of the Ruhr. The code name for the operation was "Mahseer" and the town of Krefeld was the target. Krefeld, with a population of 170,000 was a modern industrial town on the west bank of the Rhine, about three miles from the river itself and fifteen miles northwest of Dusseldorf.

Krefeld was the largest producer of high-grade steel in Germany, and the steel was sent to Krupps where it was used in the manufacture of aero engines and machine tools. In addition to its steel industry, it had been famous since the seventeenth century for the manufacture of silks, which during the war was being used to manufacture parachutes. The town was also a major rail junction. It was necessary to destroy the town in order to hamper the German industrial war effort.

There were 705 aircraft in the raid. Dad was in one of the 117 Stirlings that took part alongside 262 Lancasters, 209 Hallifaxes, 105 Wellingtons, and 12 Mosquito Pathfinders leading the way.

In order to saturate the German defences, the bomber crews were instructed to make every effort to keep in a tight concentrated stream. In the time allotted for the raid, 53 minutes, it would mean an average of fourteen aircraft flying over the target every minute. The third wave of bombers, timed for 01.49 to 01.57 hours was entirely allocated to 98 Stirling's of No. 3 Group. The aircraft in which dad was a crewmember was part of this wave.

The raid took place in good visibility and the Pathfinder marking was textbook with 619 bombing the markers with more than 75% of bombs falling within three miles of the target centre.

A large fire quickly became established, and this remained unchecked for several hours. 900 acres out of a possible 1100 acres of built up areas were totally destroyed. Some 23 factories and 5,517 homes were destroyed according to German records.

The total known to have died in the bombing was 1,056 with a further 4,550 injured. 72,000 people lost their homes. Great confusion reigned for several weeks afterwards and this raid became known by the inhabitants of Krefeld as "The Terror Raid." The people were left nervous and apprehensive, but despite this no known hostility was shown towards the downed airmen who were captured.

The raid although successful came at a terrible price for the aircrews of Bomber Command. It was carried out before the moon period was over and the heavy casualties caused by the night-fighters were inevitable. Forty-four aircraft were lost, nine of which were Stirlings. Aircrew casualties were 221 confirmed killed, 41 successfully baled out and were captured, although 3 evaded capture.

Mulheim in the Ruhr Valley (22/23 June 1943)

No sooner had dad and the bombers of the Krefeld raid got home safely when the aircraft was refuelled and made ready for the next raid during the night of 23 June 1943. This time it was the congested town of Mulheim, sandwiched between Essen, Druisburg and Oberhausen which was the next target. It had not been targeted before.

The code-name for operation was "Steelhead", appropriate due to its industrial base of steel foundries, furnaces and rolling mills and with its position on one of the principle outlets of the Ruhr to southern Germany. The target was marked at 01.20 hours by eight Mosquito Pathfinder aircraft and the main force of 557 aircraft then pounded the area in three waves in a fearsome display of accurate bombing.

Dad's Stirling was in the third wave. In the later stages of the raid, the Pathfinders moved their markers to the northern edge of the town which had the effect of cutting all road and communication links with the neighbouring town of Oberhausen, with which Mulheim was linked for air raid purposes. It was then only possible for messages to be distributed on foot between the two centres and this greatly hindered fire and rescue efforts.

The centre and northern parts of Mulheim and the eastern parts of Oberhausen were severely damaged. 578 people were known to have been killed and 1,174 injured. 1,135 homes were destroyed and 12,637 damaged. German sources recorded that a large proportion of industries were severely affected." The British Post War Bombing Survey Unit estimated that this raid destroyed 64% of the town of Mulheim.

Heavy flak had been reported as moderate in the target area but intense in the defended areas which covered the immediate approaches. British Wireless intelligence reported 89 night-fighters active of which 46 made contact with the main force. Consequently, thirty-five bombers were reported missing in action, and aircrew casualties were high with 202 killed. Twenty-nine aircrews did manage to bale out and all but three who evaded capture were picked up to become prisoners of war.

Wuppertal (24/25 June 1943)

Sir Arthur Travers Harris, 1st Baronet, (1892-1984), commonly known as "Bomber" Harris by the press was Air Officer Commanding-in-Chief RAF Bomber Command and he was convinced that the relentless bombing of the industrial heartland of the Ruhr and its cities would hasten the end of the war.

With this belief fixed in his mind Harris pressed the aircrews under his command not let up but to carpet bomb the Ruhr area every night, no matter the cost in their lives or how exhausted they might be. Thus, RAF bomber crews nicknamed him "Butcher" Harris and I would not be surprised if dad shared in this sentiment, although he never said anything to mum about this.

After destroying much of Mulheim, 149 Squadron of Stirling bombers were once again tasked to bomb another city the following night. This time it would be at the Elberfeld part of Wuppertal, the Barmen half having been almost totally destroyed in a raid at the end of May. This city was situated on the River Wupper fifteen miles southeast of Essen, it covered an area of measuring two and a half miles by one mile and had a population of about 400,000.

Although not a large industrial town Barmen was still important for the production of small components that were used in the manufacture of tanks, vehicles, aircraft and guns. Other industries included tube and sheet metal works, wire rolling mills and the making of artificial silk.

Dad's crew rested up during the day on 24th June in readiness for the raid on Wuppertal in the early hours of 25 June. No doubt they all thought about the unknown terrors that they were about to confront but at least they were all still together to share what was to come. As usual, Petty Officer Jack Sutherst was in charge and he piloted the aircraft. Nigel was the navigator, but his surname is not recorded for reasons I shall explain later. Arthur Harris was the wireless operator and rear air gunner. Ronald Nash was the flight engineer who also the front-gunner, Eric Niqel Nicholson Beldon the bomb aimer.

The Stirlings of 149 Squadron joined Stirlings from other squadrons making a total of 98 en route to their target. With them merged 251 Lancasters, 171 Halifaxes, 101 Wellingtons and 9 Pathfinder Mosquitoes, making a total of 630 aircraft destined to bomb the Elberfeld part of Wupperta. The Barmen half of the city had been almost totally destroyed in a raid at the end of May.

Pathfinder marking was accurate and the bombing of the Main Force went well until later on when some creep back occurred causing bombs to fall in the western areas of the Ruhr. Despite this, serious damage was caused to the town with post-war British survey records estimating that 94% of Elberfeld was destroyed during this one raid.

German records show that more bombs fell on Elberfeld than had fallen on Barmen in the earlier May raid. 171 industrial premises and about 3,000 houses were destroyed. 53 industrial units and 2,500 houses were severely damaged. Known deaths totalled over 1,800 with 2,400 injured, although the final toll will never be known. Many were reported as missing.

Post-war British estimates 94% of Elberfeld destroyed by this raid but it had not without loss for the bomber crews. Thirty-four bombers were shot down, ten of which were Stirlings.

Gelsenkirchen (25/26 June 1943)

The next night, 26 June 1943, the operational code-name for the raid on Gelsenkirchen was "Ferox" and zero hour was set for 01.20 hours. The main industrial target was the Nordstern synthetic-oil plant and 473 bombers took part in the raid. It was a disaster from the start.

The target was to be marked by seven of the twelve Oboe Mosquito's despatched, four using sky marker flares. However, the fourth Mosquito reached the target area late and consequently many of the main force crews bombed before the first sky markers had ignited, and many between the gap of the 3rd and 4th Pathfinder Mosquito flare loads

To make matters worse, five of the Pathfinder Mosquito's were unable to mark the target due to equipment failures. As a consequence, the raid was not a success. Although coal production was affected for a time, damage to industrial premises amounted to 20 being hit of which 4 suffered sufficient damage to halt production. No large fires were reported, and only 16 people were killed. Because of the erratic marking by the Pathfinders, bombs fell on other parts of the Ruhr.

German reports state that 24 domestic buildings were destroyed and 3,285 were damaged. Solingen for example, a town nearly 30 miles from the target recorded 21 people killed and 58 injured. This raid was probably the only one where aircrew casualties, 173 killed, exceeded those who had died in the bombing. Thirty-five crewmen baled out and served out the rest of the war as POWs.

Cologne (28/29 June 1943)

Following the raid over Gelsenkirchen, dad's squadron had a respite of two days. It was a welcome break from the heat of war, but it was not to last. During the five month "Battle of the Ruhr", there had been four attacks on Cologne, all code-named "trout."

Official war art by W. Krogman of the bombing of Cologne
Picture Credit: This image is from the collections of The National Archives (Public Domain)

Dad had not participated in the first raid which took place 16/17 June when 212 aircraft targeted the city led by Stirling Pathfinder bombers. He was busy mine laying off the Brittany Coast at this time. However, dad was involved in the second raid on the city which involved 608 bombers and it did not get off to a promising start.

The weather forecast indicated that the city would probably be obscured with cloud. Consequently, the Pathfinders had to prepare a two-fold plan but in the event only 7 of the 12 Oboe equipped Mosquitoes reached the target and only 6 of these were able to drop their markers. The marking, using "sky marking" flares was 7 minutes late and then proceeded intermittently.

Despite all these setbacks, the Main Force comprising of 267 Lancasters, 169 Halifaxes, 75 Stirlings and 85 Wellingtons delivered a powerful blow and Cologne suffered its worst raid of the war. 43 industrial, 6 military and 6,368 other buildings were destroyed with nearly 15,000 other buildings damaged.

High explosive bombs seriously damaged Cologne cathedral. Unfortunately, the human toll was commensurate with this extensive damage. 4,377 people were killed with approximately 10,000 injured and 230,000 made homeless.

The bomber formation lost 25 aircraft, and three of these were Stirlings that were lost from dad's squadron. The first BF483 was lost without trace. Sgt Cooper, the rear gunner was only 17 and was amongst the youngest airmen to lose their lives on Bomber Command operations. The second aircraft BK703 was shot down by a night-fighter and crashed at Netersal, 19 miles south west of Eindhoven, Holland. The entire crew died and are buried in Woensel General Cemetery.

Stirling EE880 was also shot down by a night-fighter and crashed between Tielt and Houwaart, Belgium. Sergeant Foster, the Flight Engineer bailed out and managed to evade capture returning to England and his squadron to continue his operational tour. New Zealander Sgt Mears also bailed out and became a prisoner of war. The remainder of the crew perished. Three are buried in Houwaart churchyard while the pilot and bomb aimer has no known grave. In all 158 crewmen died, eighteen were captured and two evaded capture.

Cologne (3/4 July 1943)

Dad's squadron was among 653 aircraft which attacked Cologne's industrial area on the east bank of the Rhine on the night of 3/4 July 1943. This time the Pathfinder marking was accurate and was backed up by the heavy element of the pathfinder force which consisted of Stirlings. This allowed the main force to carry out a successful heavy attack on Cologne and this resulted in 20 industrial complexes and 2,200 houses being destroyed with many more damaged.

588 people were killed and over 1,000 injured but more importantly, 72,000 people were made homeless making it difficult for them to go to their underground industrial workplaces to support the German war effort.

The bomber stream came up against a new German unit, Jagdgeschwader 300, a Luftwaffe fighter-wing of World War II for the first time. Jagdgeschwader 300 had its origins in April 1943, when Major Hajo Herrmann, a decorated bomber pilot, advocated the use of single-seat day fighters as night fighters against the Royal Air Force (RAF) bomber offensive. He suggested that single seat fighters could operate in the bombers general target area using the light of target indicators, massed searchlights and the fires on the ground to spot their targets. These operations were tested over Berlin during May and June 1943 and codenamed Wilde Sau (Wild Boar).

The Wilde Sau technique was a method where the German pilot utilised any form of illumination available over the target being bombed - searchlights, target indictors, the glow of fires on the ground - to pick out an enemy aircraft to attack. Liaison with local flak defences was supposed to ensure that flak was limited to a certain maximum height. Above this the Wild Boar fighters were free to operate.

The bomber crews were not used to meeting fighters over a target area and it was some time before the real danger was realised. 53 of the 106 night-fighters despatched to attack the bomber stream engaged the bombers to devastating effect. 178 aircrews were killed as their aircraft fell in flames to the ground although another 39 managed to bale out, 35 of whom became prisoners of war and 4 evaded capture.

Gelsenkirchen (9/10 July 1943)

Bomber Command had decided to have another go at bombing Gelsenkirchen, having failed the first time 25/26 June 1943. Alas, the raid of 418 bombers faired no better than the last time. Oboe equipment failed to operate in five of the Mosquitoes and a 6th marked 10 miles (16 km) north of the target.

Essen (25/26 July 1943)

A force of 627 heavy bombers took part in the raid over Essene, with its main target being the Krupps Works, famous for their production of steel, artillery, ammunition and other armaments. Over 2,032 tons of bombs were dropped in the Oboe-marked attack at a cost of 37 aircraft lost. However, the raid was a complete success and was probably the most damaging raid of the war.

Over 90% of the industrial area was demolished, and the whole of the Krupps Works was obscured by fire. It was still burning twelve hours after the attack. Of the 190 workshops, 160 had been destroyed, many were completely gutted. Upon his arrival at the works the next morning, the owner Gustav Krupp suffered a fit from which he never fully recovered and was forced to hand over the running of the business to his son Alfried. Goebbels recorded in his diary "last raid....complete stoppage of production in the Krupps works," and that 800,000 people were made homeless in Essene.

Southern France (28 July 1943)

After the raid on Essene and after a short period of rest, 149 squadrons was sent on a new mission, thankfully not in the "land of no return", which was the Ruhr. Instead, the target was an armaments factory in Southern France.

In the notes that dad dictated to mum, he described what happened on that raid.

> *We also bombed an armament's factory in Southern France which the Germans had taken over. On this particular raid, we started out in daylight though we did not reach our target until dusk, as it was necessary to go the longest way round the Bay of Biscay to avoid German held territory.*
>
> *This surely was a sight to behold, whether from the ground or amongst us all in the air, for as far as one could see, behind and in front, there were planes, planes and more planes. In actual fact, about one thousand bombers in all! Usually, our missions took place at night, but we were in daylight now, so the sight could be clearly seen.*
>
> *Because of the number of planes flying on this raid, it was thought that there would be many sad and tragic losses, however in total, there were only about twenty-five losses in all which was not too great. It had been a smart move to go the longest way and obviously unexpected by the enemy; they would probably have assumed that we were making for Northern Italy which was the normal route taken for that event.*

Remscheid (30/31 July)

This was the last raid of the Battle of the Ruhr, and the target was Remscheid, a town which lies to the south of the Ruhr and was the centre of the German machine-tool industry.

Of the 273 aircraft despatched on this raid, 244 reached the target, including my dad's Stirling. 95 Halifaxes, 87 Stirlings, 82 Lancasters, 9 Mosquitoes took part in the raid. The raid lasted 25 minutes and towards the end of the bombing smoke covered most of the town while fires could be seen throughout the target areas.

Although only 871 tons of bombs were dropped, the post-war British Bombing Survey estimated that 83 percent of the town was devastated. 107 industrial buildings were destroyed; the towns industry, generally, lost 3 months' production and never fully regained previous levels. 3,115 houses were destroyed. 1,120 people were killed and 6,700 were injured. However, this success came at a price. 15 aircraft (8 Stirlings, 5 Halifaxes, 2 Lancasters) were lost, but thankfully my dad was not in one of these.

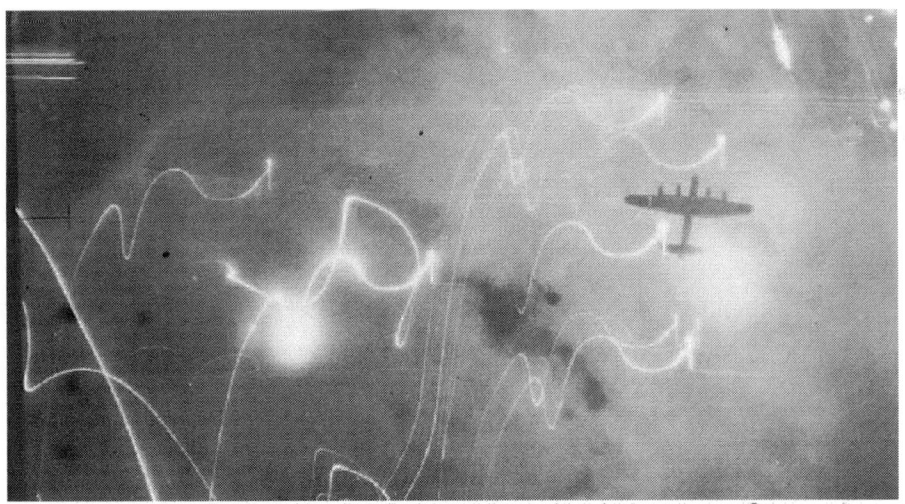

A Lancaster silhouetted against flares, smoke and explosions over a German city
Picture Credit: Photograph C 3371 from the Imperial War Museums. (Public Domain)

8 Group "The Pathfinders" and 7 Squadron

The raid on Remscheid was the twelfth and final sortie that dad and the other members of Petty Officer Sutherst's crew did with 149 squadron. After this, the crew decided that they would volunteer for operations with 8 Group "The Pathfinders." This was the elite group of bomber crews who were described by Commander in Chief Air Vice Marshal Don Bennett as,"serious, studious, meticulous - and gallant. Their contribution to victory was unique".

From its earliest operations in August 1942, the Pathfinders operated Halifax, Lancaster, Stirling and Wellington bombers and later the superb Mosquito as well. It was Bennett's wish from the outset to have an all-Mosquito and Lancaster force but this was not achieved until 1944, by which time the Pathfinders had fine-tuned a host of target marking techniques using the very latest technology of the day.

The Pathfinders job was target-marking in which a small number of pathfinder aircraft would arrive at the bombing target ahead of the main bomber force, and drop incendiaries or market the target with flares. This would provide better accuracy for the main bomber force to drop their bombs on designated targets. To help them in this important job, the Pathfinders were normally the first to receive new blind bombing aids like Gee, Oboe and the H2S radar.

For marking, the Pathfinders used a number of special "Target Indicator" (TI) markers and bombs. These ejected coloured flares or illuminated the target. Candle Aircraft, TI, Bomb, Type H were the basic indicator. About 2 feet long and about 2 inches in diametre, it sequentially ejected flare pellets that burned for 15 seconds each.

The type H was filled with alternately coloured pellets (red/yellow or red/green or yellow/green), and illuminated for about 5 1/2 minutes in total. Candles and other pyrotechnics were used as the fillings for the various Target Indicator bombs.

The early Pathfinder Force (PFF) squadrons were expanded to become No. 8 Pathfinder Group in January 1943, and No 7 Squadron based at RAF Oakington, which is were dad was assigned. I do not know what possessed my dad and his aircrew friends to volunteer for the Pathfinders, because besides being in front of the main bomber force, they would be prime targets for the Luftwaffe.

To make matters worse, instead of the 30 operational missions a crewman was mandated to do, and dad had done 12 by now, but Pathfinders had to complete 45 missions. As your number of operations increased, your odds of surviving were radically reduced and without any doubt, regardless of their skills or professionalism, the key factor to surviving was simply luck. Dad and the aircrew with whom he flew were in effect decreasing their chances of survival to the end of their term by 50%.

For one of the crewmen in dad's team, those odds and the pressure of his job on the aircraft had got to him. This was the navigator, whom dad only names as Nigel. This may be because the military authorities took a dim view on any person who displayed what was known as LMF (Lack of Moral Fibre). Little sympathy was shown to those aircrews who quite simply had given their all and could take no more. Within hours they were removed from the base, usually posted to some far away unit, demoted and put to work on menial tasks. There was no way back. Their existence on the squadron was erased, and they would not be mentioned or talked of again. Dad only talked about Nigel briefly.

> Shortly after this raid, our skipper volunteered for the Pathfinders, these were experienced crews, who myself included had already taken part in. All of my crew with the exception of the navigator joined the Pathfinders. After the last bombing raid, which was hair-raising to say the least, we didn't see Nigel our navigator again. We were told that he refused to fly again. He was quickly transferred from our base and we never heard about him again.

In hindsight, it is unfair to make judgements on men who had been pushed to a breaking point. In many ways the navigator had one of the more stressful jobs on the aircraft. His position at a table with no window and just a small light for illumination isolated him from the rest of the crew. He had to sit tight during the bomb runs and fighter and flak engagements.

In contrast the pilot was fully occupied with flying and evading the flak. The flight engineer had the engines and other systems to take care of. The bomb aimer also fulfilled the function of a gunner in the nose and along with the other gunners would have been searching the sky and if a fighter was sited he would engage it in combat. However, the navigator had to sit and take it with no outlet for his adrenaline. No wonder Nigel cracked, but in those days, his condition was not recognised for what it was, Posttraumatic stress disorder (PTSD), once called shell shock or battle fatigue syndrome.

For dad and the rest of the crew, this meant that they had a respite from flying for about a week while waiting for a replacement navigator. Canadian, Warrant Officer Carl George Baker Royal Canadian Air Force joined the crew when they moved to RAF Oakington, Cambridge, where 7 squadron was based.

If dad and his colleagues thought that they would hae a rest period, they were to to be greatly disappointed. Their posting to 7 squadron coincided with the changing from the Short Stirling to the Avro Lancaster and so the crew underwent a short conversion and familiarisation course at RAF Oakington.

This short break from night bombing operations would have been welcome for dad and his mates although the assimilation of the new aircraft and squadron would have demanded effort and concentration. So it was that dad became a Lancaster mid-turret gunner for the first time and had become a member of a Pathfinder squadron. The die was cast and there was no turning back.

Chapter 8
THE LETTER

At the beginning of September, Dad's mum received a letter from the Wing Commander of No. 7 Squadron at Oakington, dad's Pathfinder squadron. It was one that no mother would ever want to get.

Dear Mrs. Finch

It is with deep regret that I have to inform you that your son, Seargant H.S Hayward, did not return from an operational flight on the night of 30th/31st August, 1943, and has been posted as missing.

The aircraft of which your son was rear gunner was detailed to attack a target at Munchen-Gladbach, but, as the procedure for operational flights is radio silence, we are unable to provide details of what may have happened.

During the time this crew was with us it had become very popular, and impressed us all by its efficiency and determination. We have no doubt that they will have given a very good account of themselves, and there is the possibility that they are all safe.

In closing, may I extend to you my sympathy and that of the whole Squadron at this anxious time, and I trust that we shall receive better news very soon.

Sincerely
Wing Commander

Dad's Grandfather, Mother, Sisters and Bothers all prayed for him when they received the letter to say that he had been shot down and was missing. As you can imagine it was a very worrying and sad time for them not knowing if dad was alive or dead.

There was a glimmer of hope, though. It was possible that dad had survived, and this thought gave some solace to dad's family. Then weeks later, another letter, which had been forwarded to the airbase by the Red Cross in Germany, brought great relief.

Dad had escaped from the burning plane, the only survivor of his crew. He had parachuted out to safety, captured and was now interned in a prison of war camp at Muhlberg where he would remain until near the end of the war when on 23 April 1945 the Red Army liberated the camp. Many a tear flowed on that day when the news arrived on dad's escape from death.

Squadron Avro Lancaster
Picture Credit: Colourised by Fred Harding, Avro Lancaster Mk 1 Expired Crown Copyright

I have been able to piece together some of my dad's operations while he was in the Pathfinder Squadron. He says that he carried out approximately eighteen missions from RAF Oakington. One of these was the raid on Peenemunde. Official records describe the raid as an attack by RAF Bomber Command on a German scientific research centre at Peenemunde on the night of 17/18 August 1943.

The primary objective was to kill as many personnel involved in the research and development of the V-weapons as possible, by bombing the workers' quarters. Secondary objectives were to render the research facility useless and "destroy as much of the V-weapons, related work, and documentation as possible."

Operation Hydra, as it was called, would consist of three waves. But first a decoy raid would be made on Berlin by Mosquito bombers (operation whitebait).

Eight Pathfinder Mosquitoes of 139 (Jamaica) Squadron flew to Whitebait (Berlin) to simulate the opening of a Main Force raid. By imitating the typical pathfinder marking of the target, it was expected that German night fighters would be lured to Berlin.

At 22:56 British Double Summer Time (scheduled for 23:00), the first Mosquito was over Whitebait. Each Mosquito was to drop eight marker flares and a minimum bomb load. The trick worked, and night fighters were held back to support Berlin, ensuring that there were fewer in number to attack the main force on its way to Peenemunde, Denmark.

Fighter Command also provided 28 Mosquito and ten Beaufighter intruders from 25, 141, 410, 418 and 605 squadrons in two waves, to attack Luftwaffe airfields at Ardorf, Stade, Jagel, Westerland and Grove, to catch night fighters taking-off and landing. Eight Handley Page Halifaxes exploited the full moon to fly supply sorties to Europe, some to the Danish resistance movement, covered by the flight of the Main Force. Five Typhoons, two Hurricanes, a Mustang and a Whirlwind were to operate just across the English Channel.

The nature of the raid on Peenemunde was not revealed to the aircrews; in their briefing, the target was referred to as developing radar that *"promises to improve greatly the German night air defence organisation."* To scare aircrews into making a maximum effort, Order 176 emphasised the importance of the raid: *"If the attack fails... it will be repeated the next night and on ensuing nights regardless, within practicable limits, of casualties."*

The main attack took place at midnight of 17 August 1942.The night's sky was clear and there was a full moon. However, when the aircrafts got over Peenemunde, there were some clouds over the site and the first bombs missed their target. One-third of the aircraft in the wave bombed a forced labour camp at Trassenheide and killed at least 500 enslaved workers before the accurate markers on the housing estate drew the bombing onto the target. The AA guns opened fire and even the ship off-shore's flak opened fire, but still, there were no fighters to be seen.

About 75 per cent of the buildings where the scientists lived at Peenemunde were destroyed but only about 170 of the 4,000 people attacked were killed, because the soft ground muffled bomb explosions and air raid shelters in the estate had been well built. Even so, Dr Walter Thiel, the chief engineer of rocket motors and Dr Erich Walther, chief engineer of the rocket factory, were killed.

The second wave of 113 Lancasters, 6 Pathfinder Shifters and 12 Pathfinder Backers-Up began at 12:31 a.m. to destroy the V2 works, in two buildings about 300 yard long. The pathfinders had to move the marking from the first wave targets to the new ones, which had never been tried before.

Just before the first wave finished bombing, the Pathfinder Shifters would aim their red target indicators at the green indicators dropped by the first wave backers-up, ensuring that their red markers would land on the new aiming point, a mile short of the previous one. The green markers had been laid accurately, but one Pathfinder Shifter dropped 75 miles short and three overshot by the same distance. The last shifter marked accurately and Searby warned the second wave to ignore the misplaced markers.

The bombing hit a building used to store rockets, destroying the roof and the contents. During the attack, a high wind blew target markers eastwards, leading to some aircraft bombing the sea.

The third wave was made up of 117 Lancasters of 5 Group and 52 Halifax and nine Lancaster bombers of 6 Group, which attacked the experimental works, an area containing about 70 small buildings in which the scientific equipment and data were stored, along with the homes of Dornberger and his deputy Wernher von Braun. The wave arrived thirty minutes after the beginning of the attack; the crews found smoke from the bombing and the German smoke screen covered the target, clouds were forming and night-fighters decoyed to Berlin had arrived. However, it was too late, the bombers had achieved their goals.

Sadly, despite the decoy efforts, 40 bombers were shot down and 215 aircrew were killed. There was also collateral damage as several hundred enslaved workers in the nearby Trassenheide labour camp were killed by misplaced bombs. Nonetheless, the raid was a success. Two senior V-2 rocket scientists were killed, prototype V-2 rocket launches were delayed for about two months, testing and production was dispersed and the morale of the German survivors was severely affected.

Somewhere among the Pathfinder bombers leading the raids over Peenemunde dad's Lancaster was in the thick of it. He said in the notes that mum had written:

> *Around about the time of August 1943, we carried out a very important raid on Peenemunde, this was a factory on the Baltic Coast in Germany where V1 and V2 rockets were being made, there were about nine hundred planes on this mission, Lancasters and Halifaxes mainly.*

We were later told that this was a very successful raid, as most of the factory was destroyed and this certainly slowed up the production of these hideous weapons.

Dad also said that following the raid on Peenemunde, "we carried out more raids over Berlin and the Rhur until being sent on what was to be our final operational trip, a German twin-town called "Munchen-Gladbach". My son Adam takes up the story as to what happened from what his grandad told him and what was recorded in the notes that mum had accumulated from what dad had said to her.

During this operation over Munchen-Gladbach, my Grandad had been detailed to operate as rear gunner instead of his usual place as mid upper gunner, this was because a new recruit had joined named George Wallace and he was trained to be a mid upper turret gunner.

This move saved my Grandads life. So on August 31st 1942, whilst on operational duty over "Munchen-Gladbach", my Grandad's plane was shot down by a Messerschmitt 110 night-fighter, which was firing cannons. The cannons hit the petrol tank, and my Grandad's plane went up into a verticle dive and was on fire.

My Grandad opened the turret doors, rotating dead stern, but he had to claw his way upward, as gravity was pulling him back, due to verticle dive. His parachute was about three feet six inches behind the turret in a rack.

Grandad managed to clip it onto the harness, which he was already wearing. After achieving this, he more or less fell back into the turret, as sliding doors were already open, he then rotated the turret on the beam and then pushed his feet up onto the guns and kicked himself out of the turret.

All of my Grandad's mates perished; there was nothing he could do, no time. He saw one man in the middle of the aircraft. He could have been the mid upper gunner, and he was standing surrounded by flames. There were just two tiny circular windows in the small doors between my grandad's mate and himself. This was the second time my Granddad believed a Guardian Angel to watching over him. If he had been carrying out his normal duties as the mid upper gunner, he would not have survived this operation.

Dad jumped from the burning plane, no one could ever imagine how he felt knowing that he would never see his mates again, knowing that he could not save any of them. Those thoughts were to stay with him for the rest of his life.

My Granddad landed in a German field in the dark with only one boot on. He managed to hide for two days and nights. Walking by night and sleeping during the day. He had no food during this time. He was eventually found in a barn by a German couple who were farmers. They held a shotgun to Grandad whilst the German police were called. Grandad was taken to a prisoner of war camp in Muhlberg where he was to spend the next 20 months.

I was later to learn that the prisoner of war camp where dad was incarcerated was Stalag IV-B, one of the largest prisoner-of-war camps in Germany during World War II. Stalag is an abbreviation of the German Stammlager ("Main Camp"). It was located 8 km (5.0 mi) north-east of the town of Mühlberg in the Prussian Province of Saxony, just east of the Elbe river and about 30 mi (48 km) north of Dresden.

What happened to Dad during his internment at Stalag IV-B was something he would not talk about and never passed on what he went through during those dark days of his life. He only talked a little about the happiness he felt when he was eventually freed from captivity by the Americans, which is understandable.

I can only deduce that during the long periods of inactivity in the camp dad brooded over what had happened to his aircrew friends that when down with his plane. The sight of seeing them engulfed in flames and the sounds of their screams gave him nightmares after the war. That and the deprivations he encountered, the sights he saw as a POW in the crowded camp, no doubt added to my dad's psychological burden. So when he was finally freed in 1945, he was but a shadow of his former self, both physically and psychologically.

It goes without saying that when dad died in March 2000 it was a time of great grief for me and all the family. Even more so when mum showed me the notes, she had written over the years during their marriage over the conversations she had with dad over his war time experiences. I was tearfully moved to find out more about the missing part of dad's life that he had not shared with her.

With this in mind I employed aviation historian Graham N. Osborn, who lived at Boscombe, near Bournemouth in 2001 to find out what he could about dad from the official records of his military history and if possible, anything he could about dad's experiences at Stalag IV-B. The information that I now relate in the next chapter is what Mr. Osborn had researched and documented in a report which he presented to me in January 2002, a few months before another tragedy hit the family, the death of my mother.

It is only now that I have, with the help of my cousin, Fred Harding, been able to put together this book of my dad's story and, as part of that I believe Mr. Osborn's report, which now follows, is an important historical document that should be recorded for posterity. It provides first-hand experiences of POWs at Stalag IV-B where my dad was incarcerated, experience that he himself would have went through.

Chapter 9
INSIDE STALAG IV-B

Entrance to Stalag IV-B
Picture Credit: Colourised by Fred Harding, (Public Domain)

Dad's experience as a prisoner at Stalag IV-B was something he was unwilling to discuss with his family. This is understandable. For him those were dark days best forgotten and having married my mother and surrounded by his three growing children, he was happy.

After the war and after working for the Metropolitan police for a short period, dad decided to train as a carpenter; I think he had had enough of the rules and regulations associated with military/policing style work and thought carpentry would be something completely different, this was before I was born. I only ever knew him as a carpenter but in my adult life I came to appreciate the incredibly difficult but interesting life my dad had experienced.

We found out through research the extent of dad's bravery and hardship not just during the war but during his childhood. By the time I had discovered most of his history, dad had already passed away and it is one of my biggest regrets that I did not fully appreciate what a very special man he was when he was alive.

When dad died in 2000 and reading the notes that my mum had written over the years, I felt compelled to find out more about dads military career. I sent a letter to the RAF and they were really helpful and replied and this was my starting point of uncovering his story. That next stage was to find an historian who was interested in military history; I employed aviation historian Graham N. Osborn, who lived at Boscombe, near Bournemouth in 2001 to carry out some research for me, to find out more about dad's military record and anything that might shed some light on dad's POW experience.

OVERVIEW

Few photographs have survived of Stalag IVB. I have knowledge of aerial photographs of all the known Prisoner of War Camps in Germany and the occupied countries that were taken by highflying allied photo reconnaissance aircraft throughout the period of hostilities. Classified as Secret they were shown to bomber and intruder crews before raids in an effort to mitigate the possibility of munitions falling on our own men.

Sadly this was not always the case particularly towards the end of the war when the Germans started moving prisoners into known target areas in the hope of discouraging the bombing.

Muhlberg followed the pattern of other POW Camps consisting of several rows of large barrack huts each one designed to house about 200 prisoners although there is evidence to suggest that on occasions as many as 500 would be accommodated in each hut. At its peak in 1944 intelligence reports indicated that 14,000 PoWs were being held at Muhlberg.

Stalag IV-B was one of the largest POW camps in Germany
Picture Credit: J.H. Adam, Stalag IV-B6 - Museum, Public Domain (Wikipedia Commons)

The huts were of wooden planking construction. They did not have a cavity wall or interior cladding. They would therefore be similar in construction to your average garden shed although on a much larger scale. Heating was provided by coke or wood fired stoves, probably two or three arranged down the central isle.

By late 1944 fuel had become very scarce and throughout the winter of 1944/45 the inmates suffered from extreme cold resulting in many fatalities. This was particularly so in the case of Russian and Italian prisoners who were more harshly treated than their British and Americans counterparts. Arranged down each side of the hut were three tiered wooden bunk beds upon which was placed a straw filled mattress. This "luxury" was not afforded to Russian prisoners.

A cook house and latrine block would complete the arrangements for the prisoners although in some camps where conditions were more relaxed a building was set aside for recreational facilities. This was not the case at Muhlberg. The vast majority of prisoners at Muhlberg were of Russian and Ukraine extraction and the Germans were particularly harsh in the treatment of Soviet POWs and this had a knock on effect for the other nationalities.

Sanitation and the prevention of disease was also a problem. Towards the end of the hot summer of 1944 there was an outbreak of Typhus at the camp and yet the reaction of inmates to this was characteristically phlegmatic.

POW 259924 Fg/Off Alexander Wood . Stalag IVB. 9 September 1944

" ...Yes, the scare which stopped our entertainment was Typhus, quite bad enough, what?"

Sgt Hayward, now identified as POW 222713, would have been transported to Muhlberg in an enclosed cattle truck, this was standard German practice, and was not considered to be harsh or degrading by the authorities. In some ways he was fortunate that this movement probably took place before the onset of winter when the journey would have been much more unpleasant. Although I have been unable to find any direct references to Sgt Hayward's time in captivity it is possible to accurately describe this period from other contemporary reports and letters sent home by inmates.

On arrival at Muhlberg he would have undergone yet one more indignity, that of the camp haircut. A kind of "sheep shearing" machine with a hand wheel at one end of a flexible tube and a set of clipper shears at the other was operated by two men. With this primitive tool one turned the wheel while the other cut hair from the next mans head. All ended up as bald as coots.

Prisoners were allowed to write one letter per month but this had to be to a direct relative who shared the same surname. All mail was censored both by the inmates themselves and their German hosts. Incoming and outgoing mail was dependent on the International Red Cross for delivery and as the war progressed this service started to break down. This had a debilitating effect on morale.

Contemporary war films often depict a cavalier attitude by prisoners towards their predicament and while there is no doubt that certain individuals were disposed towards this genre. However, the majority of prisoners were resigned to long hours of boredom. The maintenance of morale and a sense of optimism was therefore a continuing priority for the officers and senior NCOs who were charged with the day-to-day discipline of the men. To help administer this situation the allied prisoners introduced a prison camp disciplinary code. This covered many aspects of day to day camp life to ensure that discipline and moral were maintained. Overt pessimism was a punishable offence under this code.

The Germans particularly in the case of prisoners from eastern Bloc countries fragrantly ignored the Geneva convection restricting the use of prisoners for war related work. However, the British and Allied POW's were required to work on land or other food production work. In some cases there" is evidence that they were also required to work on clearing and repairing bomb damaged areas.

In most camps the summer weather caused a huge increase of every kind of flying, crawling and creeping vermin imaginable. Within the crowded conditions of the camps dysentery was endemic and after an outbreak of typhus amongst Russian prisoners the fear of the disease spreading beyond the confines of the camp concerned the Wehrmacht high command. At Stalag IVB the Commandant decided to fumigate the huts. The Kriegies were turned out for a couple of hours while the huts were sealed and then fumigated with Zyklon B gas. It was most effective and the men returned to their huts to find the floor littered with the dead bodies of rats, mice and numerous insects. Zyklon B was the gas used at Auschwitz and Bergen Belsen.

A large parade area was at one end usually leading towards the main gate as this gave the guards an uninterrupted field of fire from the perimeter towers. At least two and sometimes more high barbwire fences surrounded the whole of the complex. Watch towers were positioned at regular intervals around the perimeter and it was normal practice for regular patrols, usually with dogs to walk around the enclosure created by the dual fence. This gap was also a kept clear of all other obstructions thus affording a clear field of fire for the guards. Accommodation for the guards and the camp commandant was outside the main prison compound although administrative facilities and other related buildings were arranged within the main perimeter fence.

As already explained, due to the large numbers of Soviet prisoners held at Muhlberg, conditions were more harsh than at other similar facilities. Much of this attitude was attributable to the camp commandant who was particularly punitive. For example, in the early summer of 1944 a British Corporal was summarily executed for stealing some strawberries from the German guards.

Parcels from home, via the Red Cross, were allowed and eagerly anticipated by the inmates, however, as the war progressed it became commonplace for such items to fail to reach the intended prisoner. As to if this was intentional on the part of the Germans or just another indication of the deteriorating social and administrative situation brought about by the advancing allied armies and incessant bombing is a matter of conjecture.

British Prisoner 222689 F/Sgt Elwell. Stalag IVB. 3 December 1944.

"We heard today that the March April and May clothing parcels were all missing, so I can kiss my boots goodbye."

At vary late stage in my research documents came to light that have enabled me to document the entire period of Sgt Hayward's internment. The information is very general in nature although some specific events such as attempts at escape, camp entertainment etc. are covered. To list all of this in diary form would take a considerable period of time and quit frankly would make for tedious reading. However, it is worth looking at some of these entries to assist in help the understanding of this period in Sgt Hayward's life.

SURVIVING PURGATORY

End November 1943
Weather cold and damp.

A large party of prisoners was sent to the railway sidings at Muhlberg to collect a delivery of Red Cross parcels. It was noted that the adults in the streets of Muhlberg watched the truckloads of Kriegies (Prisoners) with apathetic lack of emotion. The children, however, were openly antagonistic, spitting and swearing and throwing things at them. The guards did little to prevent this from happening .

15 December 1943
Bitterly cold day. Frost over night. Light snow falling.

At the morning Appell (Parade) the Kommandant addressed the assemble Kriegies and warned them that if the Russians were not stopped in their advancer into Germany then they would overrun all of Europe. He then asked for volunteers for a military unit to be called The Legion of St George to fight the communists. There were no takers.

In early January 1944 Stalag IVB received its most remarkable intake of prisoners. Four hundred Polish women who had been captured in Warsaw were moved into the adjoining compound to the British prisoners. Many prisoners had not seen a woman in over two years and to many, these women all looked like Betty Grable or Rita Hayworth. This was patently not the case.

14 March 1944

Sgt Hayward was promoted to F/Sgt in accordance with the terms of his service. He would have been notified of the promotion by the German authorities who themselves would have been advised through the Red Cross acting as the protecting power.

19 March 1944
Mild, dry and cloudy with a strong wind from the southwest.

A South African in hut 59 committed suicide by hanging himself.

20 March 1944
Still windy and now snow falling.

The Italian prisoners put on a show for their British counterparts. An Italian tenor sang and was extremely well received.

26 March 1944
Mild but overcast morning.

Snow still on the ground and more fell during the afternoon.

Germans refuse permission for church service. Passion Sunday. No coal issue and huts very cold. One stove for cooking only

28 March 1944
Spring is in the air.

Sunny morning although heavy frost overnight. Snow still on the ground.

Two prisoners shot during the night. One was caught trying to steal coal and a sentry shot another as he put his head out of the window to watch the air raid that was in progress at 0300 hours. Third night in a row for air raids.

29 March 1944
Raining hard.

Roll call held in the huts. Polish prisoners moved from camp. Destination unknown, but they were not seen again. Security very tight. Germans are getting very edgy about air raids and issue a warning that exuberance on the part of the prisoners will lead to more shootings .

5 April 1944
Cloud and rain.

Hot baths for British Prisoners. During a Rugby match a Frenchman drove a horse and cart across the pitch running over one of the players causing him serious injury. The Frenchman had to be rescued by the Germans as he was about to be lynched. Food parcels arriving at the camp but most have been damaged by fire, further evidence of air raids. Food parcels that arrived last week had all been looted, probably by the local population. Food and fuel now in short supply for the German people.

13 April 1944
Spring day.

Volleyball competition. The Germans have started standing men against the wire for periods of up to two hours or being late on roll call. This punishment had, until recently, been reserved only for the Italian and Russian POWs.

16 April 1944
Another fine day.

Rude awakening at 0600 instead of 0730 hours. Germans looking for escaped prisoners. Camp swarming with guards all day.

30 April 1944
Bright morning.

Night curfew now starts at 2100 hours. Nasty accident during the afternoon. Junkers 88 fighter bombers from a nearby airfield frequently "buzzed" the prison camp. On this day the inevitable happened when one came too low and hit two RAF men playing football. Both were killed. The aircraft then hit the fence tearing it out but managed to keep flying.

1 May 1944
May Day. Breezy and cloudy.

Cigarette ration issued. Russian female prisoners, who had for the past few days been cavorting around their compound in their underwear, or less, due to the heat, have returned to more substantial dress. The numbers of prisoners taking a stroll by the wire has noticeably diminished.

At a meeting this morning between senior British RAF officers and the Camp Commandant to discuss yesterdays incident with the low flying aircraft the Commandant said that the pilot had been arrested and that he expected him to be severely punished. Continuing he said that he regarded prisoners to be soldiers not PoWs and that the tragedy had caused him great distress. A full enquiry was to be held and statements were required from all witnesses.

The Red Cross were to be informed and he promised that he would notify the camp as to the outcome of the enquiry. Luftwaffe High Command had ordered an immediate halt to all unauthorised low flying.

5 May 1944
Dull and wet.

Germans say that non delivery of mail is due to letters containing too many printed pages, too many letters being written etc. Prisoners asked to remedy the situation by writing to family members and requesting shorter letters.

More air raids. Bombs now falling closer to the camp as the Allies attack nearby airfields and military installations. Air Raid trenches being dug on the football and rugby pitches, but they will hold no more than 200 prisoners each. Camp houses nearly 12,000. Bath day for British POWs. The first in three weeks.

24 May 1944
Very bright sunny day.

Two RAF officers attempted to escape along with 13 Dutch officers. They were using forged l/D cards and were taking advantage of a transfer of prisoners outside the wire. They were caught.

28 May 1944
Hot and sunny after early morning mist.

Prisoners spent much of the day watching bombers fly high overhead as the American Air Force flew deep into the heart of Germany. Hour's later strips of thin silver paper came fluttering to earth and littered the compound. This was strips of window.

The Russian women are displaying themselves again and so are the German women from the nearby town who have taken to promenading outside the wire in summer frocks which rise high in the wind. The German guards are reluctant to take action, presumably they to enjoy the display.

29 May 1944
Whit Monday. Cloudless sky.

Food parcels issued two per man for British prisoners. Russians less fortunate. Ground now very dry and dust is getting everywhere. British fighter crash-lands close to the camp. The pilot, who was injured, is brought straight to the compound. Despite the heavy guard presence he manages to tell of the latest developments. Invasion imminent.

6 June 1944 Cloudy with rain.

D Day.

21 June 1944
Bright sunny day.

Girls parading once more. Captain Brown, Sussex Regiment shot while trying to escape through the wire in D compound. Despite he shortages and privations at Muhlbergt, the Kriegies found initiative and energy to form a camp amateur dramatics society(CADS). Other clubs a and organisations flourished, often based on the country of origin of the prisoners. It became he practice for club members to sport a badge, fashioned from tin, to represent their particular club.

24 June 1944
Cold north wind, cloudy

Guards turn out in force to round up late comers to morning roll call. About 100 are rounded up and made to stand by the wire. It is very cold and their colleagues bring them overcoats and hot mugs of tea, some even change places with them when the guards are not looking. Fatigue duty for all British prisoners.

27 June 1944
Dull with thunder.

Rations are to be cut and all the Italian prisoners are being moved from the camp over the next few days. The Red Cross in Geneva requires a list of all prisoners held in the camp so that unclaimed mail can be cleared. The Germans issue a warning about trying to retrieve balls that go through the wire. Sentries are to be requested to retrieve the article. They say it would be silly to jeopardise life over such a trivial matter.

28 June 1944
Cloudy and close.

Potato ration now 2,100 grams per week a reduction of 42%. Bread issue now to last three days.

3 July 1944
Warm sunny day after early morning mist.

British food parcels arrive, plus wo trailers containing clothing, boots and a piano. The concert party are delighted.

4 July 1944
Brilliant sunshine.

American independence day and the American prisoners put on baseball and American football match. All are invited to watch.

5 July 1944
Heavy overnight rain. Dull with thundery showers.

Extra guards on duty as they have been tipped off that there may have been a tunnel dug. Nothing was found.

20 July 1944
Misty morning then sunny periods with thunderstorms developing by late afternoon.

A search is made in several huts during the morning. All illicit electrical fittings, brewers, dartboards, uncensored books papers and notes are taken. Floors are taken up. Three British prisoners put in solitary confinement. One for keeping a diary, another for having excess money and a third found with ammunition in his pocket.

24 July 1944
Cloudy and cold.

Two Russian Officers were shot during the night trying to escape. Food rations now contain rotten potatoes and mouldy bread.

14 August 1944
Hot and Sunny

Dust everywhere. The camp 'swap shop' was broken into last night and tea, coffee, cocoa, chocolate and cigarettes to the value of 6,993 cigs were stolen. Although prisoners received money, in the form of local currency from the protecting power, the main camp currency was cigarettes.

12 September 1944
Cold night with cold easterly wind all day.

The CADS put on a show "Kreigie Kocktail" described by many as the best yet. Cricket knockout competition started.

13 September 1944
Cold and sunny.

The French put on a show, "Musique et Danse" an exceptionally good performance of classical music and dances. Fraternisation between the different nationalities, while not being actively encouraged seemed to be tolerated by the Germans. There was much international rivalry and camp entertainment was just one area where the differing nations tried to out do each other. It has to be said that not everyone understood the British sense of humour!

15 October 1944
Cloudy morning but brighter in the afternoon.

A full loaf of bread was stolen from one of the British huts. It is believed that the person responsible is Russian. A new commandant arrived and he issued orders that all German Officers were to be saluted and that he expected all inmates to behave as disciplined soldiers. There followed an issue of food parcels and personal mail, much of which had been stored for many weeks.

Petty theft was rife within the camp. With many men on the point of starvation, they were pushed to do things they would probably never consider under normal circumstances. If a culprit was caught, he could expect harsh treatment from both sides although prisoners tended not to be handed over to the German authorities. as it was possible they would be executed.

29 October 944
Cloudy and slush underfoot.

Another 1,000 polish women, mainly young girls arrived in the transit part of the camp. They were all strip searched in the open compound but most prisoners turned away at this degrading spectacle.

31 October 1944
Overcast with rain.

Camp commandant issues new orders with regard to treatment of Polish female prisoners following complaints from British and Americans. He suggested that as they arrived with little more than what they stood in, perhaps help could be offered to make life more comfortable for them. Collection of clothing and food donated to the Polish female prisoners from all sections of the camp

13 November 1944
Cold and cloudy

Further food reductions to be made. Rations now below starvation level with each man receiving 350 grams of potatoes or fresh vegetables per day. Prisoners ordered to wear white triangle painted on all outer clothing.

21 November 1944
Gale force winds and rain.

More than half of the Polish girls were transferred from the camp today. They had contributed much to the lightening of a dreary life and there was much remorse at their departure. Many were concerned as to their future, as under the ever watchful eye of the British and American prisoners the camp commandant had ensured their safety and fair treatment.

23 November 1944
Rain all day with strong winds. Cold.

Finding somewhere dry and out of the wind, even in the huts becomes a priority. A truck arrives with stores for the prisoners. Hopes are raised but quickly dashed when they find it consists of boot polish and brushes, toothbrushes, insecticide and musical instruments. Great hilarity returns when one large box is found to contain women's silk underwear and Christmas decorations. The general consensus of opinion is that they will all be put to good use particularly as a new production by the CADS is planned for Christmas.

14 December 1944
Snow with slush underfoot.

Christmas parcels arrive for some prisoners. British and American prisoners are said to number 7,668

24 December 1944
Extremely cold.

Props for pantomime are being prepared. The Germans say they will allow a carol service for all the men providing that they behave in an orderly and disciplined way. Allied senior officers give their word that this will be the case.

25 December 1944
Clear but very cold.

Reveille at 0700 and roll call at 0800 hour. Huts decorated and every effort is made to make the festive spirit effective. Christmas lunc consisted of vegetable broth and a pudding made from bread sugar and honey. An issue pf one half of German beer was made to each inmate. The Russians did not do as well. A further 1,300 Russian prisoners arrived during the day to add to the already overcrowded conditions.

1 January 1945
Very cold.

No parade today which allows many a very welcome lie in. A contingent of American prisoners arrive, all are in a very bad way with many suffering from frostbite and the effects of the cold. Overcrowding in the huts is now becoming critical.

At night it is almost impossible to move with men sitting or sleeping on every bit of available floor space. The air is heavy and sanitation us becoming a serious problem.

3 January 1945
POW 270018 Flt/Sgt Compstow. Stalag IVB

"Christmas and New Year went reasonably well and I had a much better time than I had anticipated but I'm glad it's all over, the false gaiety was all too apparent, as most of us expected to be home. I say most, because like anywhere else we have our gloom club, but since the penalty for undue pessimism has become a ducking in the pool their ranks have diminished considerably!"

11 January 1945
Heavy snow.

Theft is now becoming a serious problem. Six Americans were each given 7 days detention, imposed by the British, in the cooler for stealing. Another found to have threatened another prisoner with a knife was handed over to the Germans. The Allied senior officers have decided to get tough.

Mainstreet of Stalag IV-B during Winter
Picture Credit: Lutz Bruno, Public Domain, Wikipedia Commons [CC BY-SA 3.0]

29 January 1945
More snow.

Food parcels issues are in poor supply and each one now has to supplement eight men.

During February the overcrowding was relieved to some extent when many of the Russian and Polish prisoners were moved from the camp. This allowed a redistribution of the remaining prisoners. Hot showers are reintroduced having been severely limited since November.

2 March 1945
Gale force winds.

During the day a large force of America bombers fly high over the camp on their way to Berlin. One is hit by flak. The ten-man crew all manage to bail out and two actually land within the confines of the camp. Whilst unfortunate from the airmen's point of view this incident is greeted with much glee by the inmates as fresh up to date news on the progress of the war is obtained. The prisoner strength is now put at 8,988 with food stocks for 4,710.

The Germans are being pushed back on all fronts and with the Russians advancing rapidly towards the Elbe there is noticeable change in the attitude of the guards. All escape attempts are now prohibited by the allied command as it is felt that liberation cannot be far away.

12 March 1945
Mild and overcast.

Each hut receives 7 tins of Red Cross Milk. Daily food ration now 225grams of black bread, no potatoes and thin pea soup. Six men were arrested by the Germans for stealing. Fate unknown.

The extremes to which men faced with starvation are pushed is graphically illustrated by an incident that occurred during March. A boiler full of soup was accidentally knocked over, in frenzied scramble man literally attempted to lick if from the floor.

Comment:

By early April the administrative function of the German state had all but collapsed. Muhlberg still remained in German hands but was subject to almost daily air raids although great care seemed to be taken by the attacking aircraft to avoid any munitions falling near the camp. The guards were noticeably edgy and care had to be taken at all times to avoid antagonising them. Food was extremely scarce but spirits were starting to rise as it was apparent to all that liberation would not be far away.

14 April 1945
Cold but sunny.

Comment:

F/Sgt Hayward may not have been aware of it but on this day he was promoted to Warrant Office. The necessary documentation would eventually find its way to the detaining powers but the administration functions of the Germans was now in chaos.

22 April 1945
Cloudy and cold with some rain.

Refuges are streaming past the camp. Amongst them are POA's who are diverted into the camp. A message is received from General Eisenhower ordering all POW's to stay put, maintain discipline, remain calm and not to take up arms against their captors but to await liberation.

Later in the day a large contingent of Russians arrive at the camp amongst them are about 250 officers and the other inmates hope that they are able to exert some control over the other Soviet prisoners who are becoming increasingly restless.

There is no bread ration today and water and electricity supplies to the camp have been cut. Liaison between the Camp Commandant and the British and Americans is still amicable but the other nationals are having problems with discipline which is threatening the stability of the camp. By 21.00 hours all the German guards had left including the camp commandant.

23 April 1945 St George's Day
Russain cavalry take over the camp at 07.00 hours.

Four officers on horseback ride in and in the woods close by hundreds of men on horseback can be seen.

Comment:

Stalag IV-B had now been liberated by the Soviet army. By this time 30,000 prisoners were now crowded in the camp, of these 7,250 were British. Food and hygiene facilities were at a breaking point, with tuberculoses, and typhus was common. About 3,000 prisoners had died, mainly from these diseases. They were buried in the cemetery in neighbouring Neuburxdorf, Bad Liebenwerda. Today there is a memorial and a museum commemorate them there.

At the time of the liberation, the situation could be best described as chaotic. As to what happened next in Muhlberg is not known. Records cease on the 23 April and eye witness accounts are not available.

What is known is that as each camp was liberated the inmates became the responsibility of the liberating force. Arrangements for repatriation of allied prisoners had been put in hand long before the defeat of Germany and the basic plan called for all prisoners to remain in their camps where they would be cared for prior to an orderly evacuation.

Although the camp had been liberated, the Soviet liberators held the British and American prisoners in the camp for over a month, but thankfully the Americans arrived to free them. Dad said this was a most joyous occasion and later he told us some happy stories about this time.

For example, dad told us that the Americans took the POWs in their charge into a bar and demanded of the German barman that he provide the 'best whiskey' for each man. The bar tender produced whiskey that was not 'the best' and the Americans threatened the barman with guns, the best whiskey soon appeared! One of the Americans played a piano and the men sang, it was a day to remember! Upon leaving, the Americans opened fire into the bar and fired a series of shots at the piano destroying it and probably other items in the bar too.

However, this was just a brief happy interlude in an otherwise unpleasant experience of twenty months of soul-destroying incarceration and on this dad did not wish to talk about it. Thanks to the research carried out by Mr. Osborn, now I know why.

EPILOGUE

Bomber Command, which had done so much to bring about the defeat of Nazi Germany, now found itself with a new role. The Lancaster, Stirlings and Halifaxes were used to ferry supplies out to the beleaguered and demoralized German people. Dad returned via RAF Merryfield Somerset, the exact date is unknown but by the 8 May 1945, he was admitted to the RAF hospital at Wroughton.

Dad's exact medical condition is not known, but he would be malnourished. Dysentery was endemic in the camps, and the effects of the cold would also have taken their toll.

Dad did tell us that when he returned to England he weighed little more than eight stone. It was recorded in his service book record that dad was 5ft 11 and a half inches tall. Dad was a big man, never over weight but just big and I remember that his weight was normally about 12 and a half stone. I can only imagine what he must have looked like in May 1945 upon his return to England weighing just eight stone.

Another result of dad's awful circumstances as a PWO was that a few years after his repatriation, he had to have all his teeth removed due to their terrible condition. He was only a young man then so this must have been a terrible blow. I only ever remember dad wearing dentures. It became apparent in later life that there were other health consequences for dad to bear.

Prisoner Reception Centres had been set up at various locations to receive the thousands of returning POWs. Many were in need of urgent medical attention, and so they were moved to military hospitals. The authorities also needed to interview every returning POW to establish identity, his needs and many other aspects relating to his period in captivity.

Evidence was also being collected with a view to future war crime trials and so it was imperative that all POWs should have a chance to have their say. Military discipline had to be maintained, and the reception centres were not popular as thousands of service men, who had become used to months and in many cases years of deprivation and inactivity, were rigorously reintroduced to the daily military regime.

On the 30 May 1945 dad was moved to No.106 Prisoner Reception Centre at RAF Cosford, Shropshire. Hospital facilities were available here, and it appears that he spent time within the hospital confined. Dad was discharged from the hospital at Cosford on 5 September 1945 and moved by rail to No.109 Prisoner Reception Centre Earls Colne, Essex, where he remained until 13 December 1945. On this date dad was posted to No.100 Personnel Dispersal Centre at Uxbridge, Middlesex. Ironically he had come full circle, back at the station where his RAF service had started nearly seven years earlier. It was here that dad waited for the day when he would receive his discharge papers.

Saturday, 27 April 1946 was the day and would have been a glorious day, whatever the weather. With a travel warrant to his home and with new pay and a release document in the service book in his pocket, dad walked through the main gate at the No.100 Personnel Dispersal Centre at Uxbridge for the last time.

With 75 days leave, he was still effectively in the Royal Air Force until 11 July 1946 but in reality he was now a civilian. Dad had served and survived the war, but he was to have some bad news when he got back home.

When dad returned home to his mother he learned that his grandad, who had brought him up, had died and left his property to dad, which was at Paternoster Road in Walton on the Naze, Essex.

Gladys Hayward holding her son, my dad

My Grandparents: Gladys & Harold Hayward

Upon leaving the RAF and after experiencing being so near to death during the bombing raids many times and surviving the horrors of the POW camp, all dad wanted to do was enjoy life, so the house was sold and the money quickly dwindled away.

My dad was a generous man, and I wouldn't be surprised at all that he spent a substantial amount of money on others, as a consequence, there was no long term benefit to dad financially from the property which he was later to reflect on!

Now back at home dad enrolled as a police officer. However, once qualified and operational, he decided that being a policeman was not for him, and he resigned.

Dad (on the right) as a police officer

Fortunately, at this time there was help at hand and schemes to help those who had served in the war, to obtain meaningful work and dad was deemed intelligent enough to be trained as an architect. Dad was able to draw, and his assessors thought that he had the right aptitude for the job. However, dad decided that he did not want to spend a long time studying which is what he would have had to do to train in this profession, so instead opted to do a carpentry course and this is how his career panned out as a carpenter.

One of dad's brothers lived in Railway Street in Chelmsford, Essex and so dad lodged with him for a while. It was during this period that he met my mum - Emily Gilroy, who was named after her mother, my maternal grandmother.

My mum came from a large family who originated from the county Durham, so she was a Geordie! Mum had three sisters and four brothers but one of the sisters died aged 3 weeks old when the family still lived up north.

Mum was five years old when she had a terrible accident and lost the sight of one eye when she tried to undo her boot laces with a fork, as she dug and tugged at the lace, the fork shot up and went straight into her eye. This was a terrible time for the family because apart from this awful accident, my Grandfather Jack Gilroy had no work but many children to support, he was a coal miner but work was hard to get, and so he joined the Jarrow march (5 - 31 October 1936) which was an organized protest against the unemployment and poverty suffered in the English Tyneside town of Jarrow.

My grandparents: Jack & Emily Gilroy

Grandad Gilroy travelled all the way down south to Essex where some of his extended family had moved to and ended up living in Chelmsford, Essex. He managed get work at Hoffmans in Chelmsford, which was a factory making ball bearings. Then came the war and the children were sent down south and stayed with different relatives temporarily. Mum and one of her sisters Frances stayed with one of their aunts who had one daughter; my mum told me many years later how their cousin was allowed one egg for breakfast but her and her sister were only allowed half an egg; this may seem like a small thing but it made me realize how poor most people were and how unequal society was!

Dad also came from a large family of three half brothers and four half sisters. These were half brothers and sisters because his father died when dad was six months old due to mustard gas poisoning in the first world war and his mother remarried and went on to have seven more children; dad was brought up by his grandfather, the clockmaker who lived and owned property in Walton On The Naze, Essex. It was he who left dad his house when Dad returned home after the war.

Dad moved in with one of his brothers in Chelmsford where mum now lived with her family, she was 26 years of age and dad was 34. Mum was working in a cafe when she first met dad and remembers thinking what a handsome man he was, he clearly thought the same about mum.

The year was 1954 and at this time most young people went to the dance venues that were common at the time, where everyone knew how fox trot, waltz and quick step - my dad was a great dancer and when mum and dad turned up at the same venue one evening, I think they only had eyes for each other and their romance began!

Dad was the happiest he had ever been in his life; especially after the difficult childhood he had experienced and then his time in the RAF and Prisoner of War Camp.

Mum and dad were married on 17th March 1955, and this is a picture of the happy couple. It was taken in black and white, but my cousin Fred has colourized it for me.

I was born 31 December 1955, so you could say that I was a "honeymoon baby"! We lived with my grandparents for the first few months but then my parents managed to rent their own house in Railway Street in Chelmsford where they had very happy memories of their early years together.

Colin was born on 12 March 1959 while they still lived at this address and it was here in 1963 that Paula was born.

In the mid 1960s mum and dad moved again to Swiss Avenue, Chelmsford, to be close to our maternal grandmother (nan), after grandad died. They were very happy and content 'just to be', as I think after the trauma of war many ordinary folk were just glad to be free and safe with a reasonable lifestyle.

Most of our memories of dad are probably of when we all lived in this house. When we moved there, we were aged 10, 7 and 3 respectively. It was a very happy and secure home life which mum and dad gave us. We had some wonderful traditional seaside holidays, which we all remember vividly. Every Christmas was wonderful - we were very lucky.

One holiday is particularly remembered as my brother Colin recounts. It was 1973, and we hired a boat on the Norfolk Broads. We have vivid memories of dad in his blue swimming trunks, jumping in the water and levering the boat out of the reeds on his shoulders, to the cheering and applause of onlookers. It took a while for Dad to let Colin drive the boat again - But he did!

As we grew into adulthood, mum and dad continued to support and help us in many ways. Dad was always there to help in any way he could, but we can still see him now with his carpentry tools doing various jobs in all of our homes - it didn't matter how difficult a job was dad could always fathom out how to do it! Those were happy times, but unfortunately, the trauma and privations dad suffered during the war finally caught up with him.

Me, my brother Colin and sister Paula (September 2015)

Dad was 50 years old and had been married for 15 years happy years when we realized something was wrong. Dad started having seizures. To cut a long story short, it transpired after investigation that he had epilepsy and it was thought very likely to be connected to the trauma he had experienced during the war, another problem he was gradually developing was loss of hearing and this was also attributed to his time in service. This meant that the war had resulted in long term permanent health problems for dad.

We made contact with the RAF about the situation and after further tests and investigation, it was agreed that dad should receive a full pension as a result of his health problems resulting from his time in service during the war. This was a weight of dad's mind, as he was still trying to work as a carpenter, but could not drive, and he was on medication for his epilepsy for the remainder of his life.

After our nan died, and we had all left home, mum and dad decided to move to a smaller property. They had worked hard and had purchased their previous home and were able to buy their new home in Lupin Drive, Springfield, on the outskirts of Chelmsford in 1990.

Mum and dad had some memorable years together in their new home, they had some lovely holidays together but sadly Dad's health deteriorated, and it became increasingly difficult for dad to go anywhere far.

We all tried to be there as much as possible, dad never complained. Many people visited mum and dad because it was difficult for dad to leave the house. People who could not visit phoned regularly including his brother and sisters who live a good distance from Chelmsford.

Just a few weeks before he died, his lovely sisters came on a long journey to see him. Dad's brothers came to visit him the day before he died and I know that this would have meant so much to dad.

Mum nursed dad through his illness until the end - their bond was unique, he was so lucky to have found her, and indeed, she was so lucky to have found him. She died two years later. I end this book with these words. Our parents gave us the gift of knowing that we were loved, and they were proud of us and that was reciprocated. Our dad was a very special man; his good qualities were exceptional. They will always be in our hearts and our minds and will be for evermore.

Jacqui Hayward

MEMORABILIA

Here's dad wearing all his badges, including pathfinder badge, golden caterpillar , air gunner badge

BADGES

Dad's Pathfinder Badge

This badge was awarded from November 1942 only to Aircrews of 8 Group Pathfinder Force, the same Group my dad had joined.

Dad's Catapiller Badge

The Caterpillar Club badge was presented to Royal Air Force personnel who had 'baled out' successfully wearing an Irvin parachute made by the Irvin Air Chute Company. The recipient's name was engraved on the reverse.

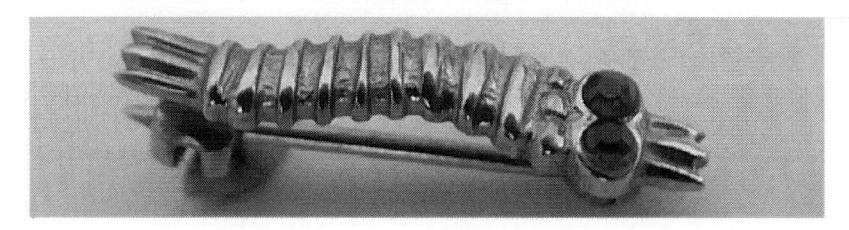

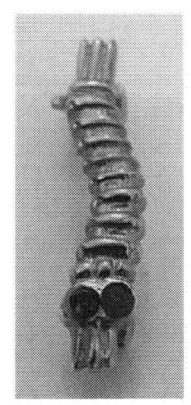

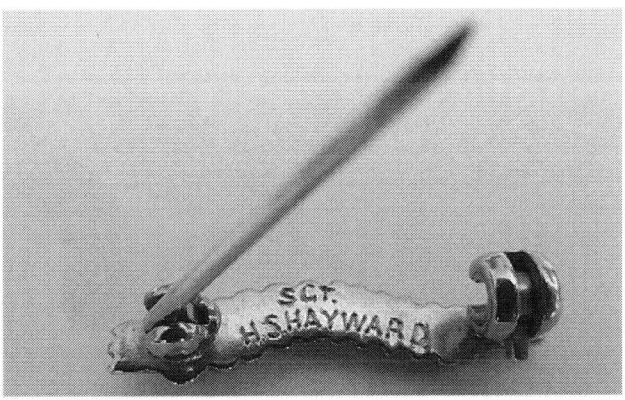

MEDALS

Defence Medal

In the United Kingdom, those eligible included military personnel working in headquarters, on training bases and airfields for the duration of the War in Europe from 3 September 1939 to 8 May 1945, and service by members of the Home Guard during its existence from 14 May 1940 to 31 December 1944.

Dad's Defence Medal (1939-1945)

Aircrew Star Medal

The Air Crew Europe Star is a military campaign medal, instituted by the United Kingdom in May 1945 for award to British and Commonwealth air crews who participated in operational flights over Europe from bases in the United Kingdom during the Second World War.

Dad's Aircrew Star

War Service Medal (1939-1945)

The War Medal 1939-1945 was awarded to subjects of the British Commonwealth who had served full-time in the Armed Forces or the Merchant Navy for at least 28 days between 3 September 1939 and 2 September 1945.

Dad's War Service Medal (1939-1945)

RELEASE DOCUMENTS

R.A.F. Form 2520A
AIRMAN

ROYAL AIR FORCE
SERVICE AND RELEASE BOOK

Rank W/O

Service Number 635675

Surname HAYWARD

Initials H.S.

Class of Release A

Age and Service Group No. 3

R.A.F. Form 2520/25

RELEASE AUTHORISATION

PART I
To be completed in Unit except when marked**.

Rank ..W/O........ Number 636628.

Initials H.S. Surname HAYWARD
(Block Letters)

To be completed at the Dispersal Centre
{ Release of the above-named airman is hereby authorised as a Class A release, and he is relegated to Class G/ of the Reserve.
The effective date of release (i.e. last day of service) is
..........1st July 46............

It is hereby certified that the above airman served in the R.A.F. on whole-time service during the following periods:

From   To
24/8/39

27 April 46
(Date of departure from Dispersal Centre)

He is granted [76] days' leave on release commencing the day following the date of departure from the Dispersal Centre

---

R.A.F. Form 2520/25
(continued)

RELEASE AUTHORISATION
(continued)

PART II
Instructions to Class B releases to report for Employment

You have been released to take up employment

Delete one if blank
{ as a ....
(Industry Group Letters;
Occupational Classification Number.................)
and are to report within seven days from your departure from this Dispersal Centre to the following Employment Exchange
....
OR
with Messrs. ....
of .... to whom you are to report within seven days from your departure from this Dispersal Centre.

You will ordinarily be required to commence work on the expiration of your leave, but you may if you desire commence at any earlier time.

PART III

[signature]
for A.O. i/c Records

Dispersal Centre Stamp.

R.A.F. Form 2520/25
(continued)

REMOBILISATION INSTRUCTIONS
(continued)

7. Do NOT bring any medals or decorations with you unless you are unable to leave them in safe custody.

8. If you have to travel by rail, use the Travel Warrant in this Book and complete the name of the Railway Station as necessary. If you do not require it, leave it in this Book which must be handed in when you report for duty.

9. If you need money for the journey the money order for 5s. in this Book may be used; present it for payment at any Post Office and produce your Identity Card and you will be paid 5s, which will be adjusted later in your account. (If you do not need the money, hand in the money order on reporting or you will be charged the 5s.).

NOTE: This money order and Warrant can only be used after a Public Notice or Proclamation has been issued; they are not valid till then.

REMOBILISATION STATIONS

10. If remobilisation or return to duty is ordered by general notice, or proclamation revoking releases or recalling the Reserve of which you are a member, a list of R.A.F. remobilisation stations will be published in the press and by public notice, showing the particular stations under code letters. Your code letter is shown below, and you should report to the station to which the code letter applies.

Your remobilisation station code letter is:—

[A]

R.A.F. FORM 2520/13

To be completed at Unit.
To be retained by Post Office.

ROYAL AIR FORCE

AVAILABLE ONLY ON REMOBILISATION BY PUBLIC NOTICE OR PROCLAMATION

To H.M. Postmaster General,

Please pay the sum of 5s. on production of his Identity Card to the airman mentioned below, if and when by Public Notice or Proclamation the R.A.F. Reserve has been called out for further Active Service before the present Emergency is declared ended. The receipt overleaf must be signed by him.

Surname HAYWARD
(Block Letters)

Christian Name(s) HAROLD SIDNEY

Service No. ......636628......

Signature of Airman ....

Stamp of Paying Post Office.

Stamp of Issuing Unit and Date.

Please read overleaf.

ROYAL AIR FORCE
CERTIFICATE OF SERVICE AND RELEASE

R.A.F. Form 2520/11

SERVICE PARTICULARS

Service Number: 635625 Rank: W/O
Air Crew Category and/or R.A.F. trade: Air Gunner
Air Crew Badges awarded (if any): Air Gunner
Overseas Service: yes 31/8/43 to 24/4/45
R.A.F. Character: V.G.
Proficiency A: Sat.
            B: Sat.
Decorations, Medals, Clasps, Mention in Despatches, Commendations, etc.: 1937/45
Aircrew Europe. Defence
Educational and Vocational Training Courses and Results: N/A

DESCRIPTION

Date of Birth: 31/7/20   Height: 5' 11"
Marks and Scars: Scar on right knee
Specimen Signature of Airman: [signature]

W/O H.S. HAYWARD
(Block Letters)

The above-named airman served in the R.A.F. on full-time service,

from 24/8/39 to 26/4/46
Last day of service in unit before leaving for release and release leave.

Particulars of his Service are shown in the margin of this Certificate.

Brief statement of any special aptitudes or qualities or any special types of employment for which recommended:—

He has a very good record of Service, and has been working very satisfactorily on this unit in the M.T. Section

Date 25.4.46   [signature]
                    Signature of Officer Commanding
                    C.F. COOKE

Notes:—
1. R.A.F. trade.—For air crew with a basic trade, show the trade in brackets after the air crew category, e.g., Pilot (Armourer).

2. R.A.F. Character during Service:
V.G. is the highest character which can be awarded in the Royal Air Force. The character assessment reflects the airman's conduct throughout the whole of his service.

3. Proficiency:
The trade proficiency headings A and B signify:—

TRADESMEN

A. Skill in his trade (applicable to airmen up to the rank of Corporal inclusive).

B. Ability as technical Warrant Officer or Non-commissioned officer, i.e., as foreman manager, foreman or supervisor in his trade.

AIR CREW PERSONNEL

A. Proficiency as pilot, navigator, air bomber, air gunner, etc.

B. Ability as a Warrant Officer or Non-commissioned officer.

Proficiency will be shown as:
 Ex. for exceptional
 Supr. for superior
 Sat. for satisfactory   } No higher or other assessment is
 Mod. for moderate   permissible.
 Inf. for inferior

4. The date to be inserted as the date of commencement of service is the date on which the airman reported for service, was called up from deferred service, called out or embodied as applicable.

R.A.F. Form 2520/14

To be detached only by Booking Clerk and exchanged for Ticket.

RECALL TO SERVICE OF AN AIRMAN ON REMOBILISATION
(To be completed in Unit except where marked**)

TRAVEL WARRANT

Charges payable by Air Ministry (F3c)   R.A.F. 2nd Class

The Directors of the Railway Company or Shipping Company concerned are hereby requested to provide conveyance for one airman by the recognised direct route to _____ **

N.B.—The airman concerned may only use this warrant if and when public notice of proclamation has been issued calling out the Reserve.

Airman's Number: 635625
Surname: HAYWARD
         (Block Letters)
Initials: H.S.

Particulars of Ticket issued, to be filled in by Railway/Shipping Co.

R.A.F. Form 2520/10
MPB 281

CLAIM FOR DISABILITY PENSION—AIRMAN

1. Surname HAYWARD (BLOCK LETTERS) 2. Service No. 626625
3. Christian Names MARLIN SIDNEY
4. Rank F/O 5. Unit/Group .... /28
6. Date of Release ....
7. Have you served in the Armed Forces before the present War and been discharged?
   ("Yes" or "No") No   If "Yes" give particulars below:—

Former Regt. Corps or Ship, etc.	Army or Official Number	Date of Discharge	Cause of Discharge	Particulars of Pension (if any) for disablement or service

8. Give particulars of your wife and children now under 16 years of age for whom you received family allowances at any time during service:—
   (a) Wife—full Christian Names ....

R.A.F. Form 2520/13

Part II to be completed at Unit.
Part III to be completed at Dispersal Centre.

PART I.
Instructions to Released Person.

MEDICAL TREATMENT AFTER LEAVING DISPERSAL CENTRE

You are now entitled to medical benefit under the National Health Insurance Acts, and a medical card telling you how to get treatment will be sent to you as soon as possible. Medical benefit includes free treatment from an insurance doctor at his surgery, or if your condition requires it, at your home, and free medicine.

If you go back to live in your old district and had an insurance doctor before you joined up you will be restored to his list if he is still in practice himself or by deputy.

If you fall ill before the medical card comes, fill in the application below and hand this book to your previous insurance doctor (or, if absent, his deputy). If you did not have an insurance doctor before you joined up or if you go to live in another part of the country, apply to any insurance doctor. You can see a list of insurance doctors at the local Post Office. Do not detach the form from the book. The doctor will do this.

Turn over for information about hospital treatment.

Form Med. 50

PART II to be completed at Unit.

Rank F/O Number 626625
Initials M.S. Surname HAYW..
(Block letters)

AUTHOR BIOGRAPHY

31st December 1955 (New Years Eve) was the day I made my entry into this world, nine months after the marriage of my parents which took place on St Patricks day 1955. I grew up in Chelmsford, Essex with my parents and younger siblings, Colin and Paula. We had a lovely childhood with wonderful Christmases and family holidays every year in UK coastal towns.

I was never an academic and was glad to leave school at 15 years old and get a job which at the time (1970) was easy to do. I applied for an insurance clerk position which coincidently happened to be located next to the first house my mum and dad live in, in Railway street, the owners of the company actually remembered my mum and dad and me as a child - they offered me the job! At age 17, I applied to Butlin's to be a redcoat, was accepted and spent two marvellous summers working at the camp in Skegness.

I married aged 20 and my son Lewis was born in 1980. This marriage did not last and in 1985, I married Julian who was at the time a dental surgeon. We went on to have 3 more children Anthony, Adam and Lauren, Julian adopted Lewis.

Despite my disappointing school life, over the years I worked towards various qualifications including completing a cert ed course at Greenwich University, which qualified me to teach in adult education. I started my own business which at the moment is still live and I also currently work for City and Guilds monitoring the delivery and assessment of qualifications. A few years ago, I was invited to do some short term work in Dubai and Saudi Arabia, which was quite an experience!

All of our children live locally and we are a close knit family with 3 wonderful daughter in laws and one son in law in waiting!!! Three of our children are married and we have three wonderful grandchildren with another due in November 2019! My hope is that this book will be read by our children, grandchildren and future generations.

DAD AND THE RADIO OF EVIL

Dad's grandfather (Edward Hayward) was a master clock maker and had a shop in Walton On the Naze, Essex, he followed a long line of ancestors - all called Edward Hayward who had also been clock makers, I have traced this information back to the early 18th century.

As a young boy, it was my dad's job to climb up to the top of the Church steeple to clean the clock under his grandfather's supervision. If it had not been for the first and second world wars, it is very likely that Harold Edward Hayward and my dad Harold Sidney Hayward would both have become part of the clock making business. Both Edward Hayward and Harold Edward Hayward are buried in the grounds of the church in Walton On The Naze where the clock was serviced.

When he was a young boy probably about 12/13, he got a job as a butchers boy, delivering meat on a bicycle, he travelled miles all over Walton, Frinton,Thorpe Le Soken in Essex and got to know quite a lot about cuts of meat and I can remember we always deferred to dad about which was the best joint to buy!

It was with the money he saved over a period of time that he purchased a transistor radio, as no entertainment was allowed in the strict Plymouth Brethren house he had been raised in. You can imagine how precious this radio was to my dad!

Unfortunately, when his grandfather(Edward Hayward) found out he had this, he destroyed it immediately as he saw it as a temptation to evil.

My Grandfather (Edward Hayward) continued to insist that dad read the bible and pray several times a day; I found a bible that belonged to my dad's own father (Harold Edward Hayward) which must have been given to him when by his grandfather (Edward Hayward) after the death of his son (Harold Edward Hayward), there are passages underlined everywhere in the bible, it is clear to me that this bible was in consistent use at least 100 years ago.

Printed in Great
Britain
by Amazon